THE MIND
AND BODY

WARWICK PRESS · NEW YORK

Endpapers: A crowd watching car racing at Daytona Beach. Previous page: Hang gliding. Top: A baby girl beginning to explore the world around her.

Above: Emi Watanabe, the Japanese-American ice-skater. Below left: Fire walkers at the Hong Kong Festival.

Published by Warwick Press, 730 Fifth Avenue, New York, New York, 10019.

First published in Great Britain by Ward Lock and Co Ltd in 1980.

Copyright © 1980 by Grisewood & Dempsey Ltd.

Printed by Vallardi Industrie Grafiche, Milan, Italy.

6 5 4 3 2 1   All rights reserved

Library of Congress Catalog No. 80-50042

ISBN 0-531-09174-0

Author   Christopher Pick

Editorial Consultants   Jack Field, Audrey Wood-Baker

Editor   Angela Wilkinson

Assistant Editor   Jane Collin

Contents

Introduction

For centuries people have tried to discover how the mind and body· work. The co-ordinated energy of the body can be demonstrated by an athlete, but the answers to questions such as how the muscles work and why they work show the complexity of the human body's structure.

The workings of the human brain are perhaps even more amazing and there is still much to discover.

"The Mind and Body" presents some discoveries already made—from why we see in color to how the memory functions.

Chapter One begins by showing how everyone is different. Chapter Two looks inside the body at the internal organs which act in the same way in all human beings. Chapter Three charts the progress of a human life from birth to death. Chapter Four shows how the body overcomes disease and how hospitals help the body to fight ill-health.

Chapter Five relates how the various senses in the body are controlled by the brain. Chapter Six describes the way in which people gradually come to understand the world. Chapter Seven shows the ways in which people learn to live with those around them.

Dozens of full-color illustrations and photographs help vividly to explain the complex workings of the mind and body. Diagrams and information boxes show clearly such things as how chicken pox is caught or why some people are deaf.

Each chapter sets out its subject clearly with the help of headings. Under each heading one main idea is explained.

If you want to check the meanings of words such as *fetus* or *utricle*, turn to the Fact Index. You will find this at the back of this book. As well as being able to look up items named in the book, you will also be able to find out more information not given in the main text.

Chapter One

Everyone Looks Different

▲ No two people in the world have the same fingerprints. Even the fingertips of identical twins are different. The unique patterns of ridges and whorls follow exactly irregularities in the underlying dermis. Even if the outer skin is damaged, the pattern does not change. This is why fingerprints are so helpful to police in identifying criminals.

Walk down a busy city street and look at the people you pass. On the outside, every single person looks different. (Even identical twins differ from each other a very little, though you would have to look harder at them than at other people.) Yet if you could strip the skin off all these people, inside you would find that everything works in exactly the same way. When you turn to chapter 2 later, you will be able to find out more about the way in which the body machine works.

So if we are all the same inside, why do we look so different on the outside? One reason is the way we have evolved since the earliest human beings lived, over two million years ago. People living in different parts of the world adapted, or changed, in different ways depending on the different conditions in which they lived. As a result, three main groups developed, each one in a different part of the world. Nowadays, however, people from all three groups live in every part of the world.

People from the same group can differ from one another a great deal. Some may be tall and thin, others short and fat. The reasons for this are partly hereditary—if your parents are tall, it is more likely that you will be tall too—and partly environmental. In rich countries, people eat better food, and more of it, and are generally healthier than people from poorer areas, and healthy people are usually taller and stronger than unhealthy ones of the same kind.

Age also makes a difference to the way people look. This becomes very clear if you compare photographs of the same person taken many years apart.

Even personality makes a difference to our appearance. Some people like to dress in bright colors, or in the height of fashion, for instance, while others prefer darker clothes or are less fashion-conscious.

▶ A group of people in a street in Israel. Though some of them may have the same skin and eye color, they are still recognizably different from one another.

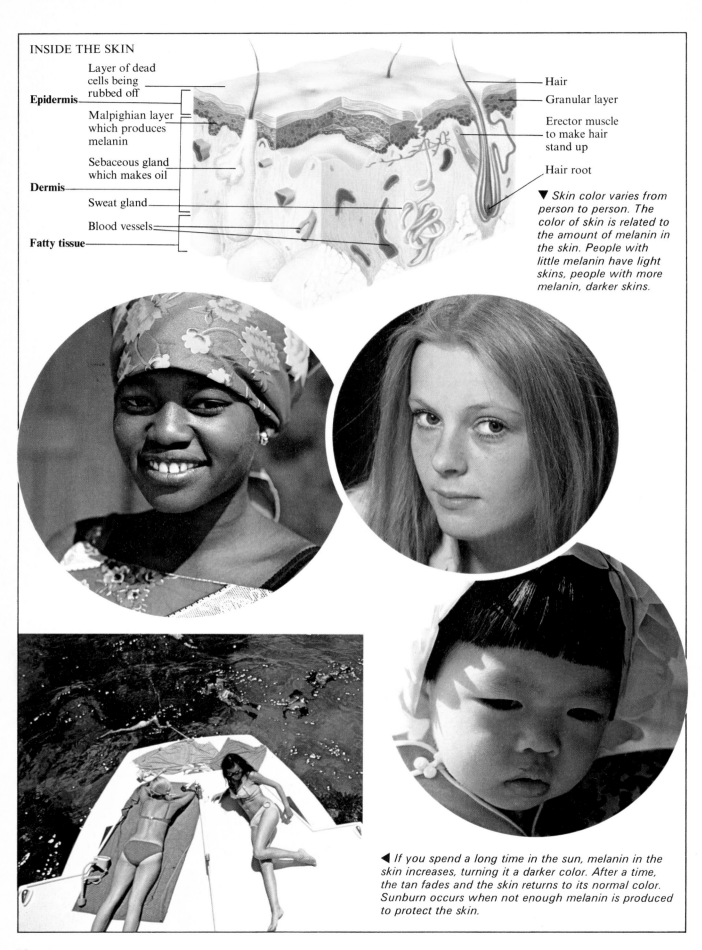

INSIDE THE SKIN

Epidermis — Layer of dead cells being rubbed off

Malpighian layer which produces melanin

Sebaceous gland which makes oil

Dermis — Sweat gland

Blood vessels

Fatty tissue —

Hair

Granular layer

Erector muscle to make hair stand up

Hair root

▼ *Skin color varies from person to person. The color of skin is related to the amount of melanin in the skin. People with little melanin have light skins, people with more melanin, darker skins.*

◀ *If you spend a long time in the sun, melanin in the skin increases, turning it a darker color. After a time, the tan fades and the skin returns to its normal color. Sunburn occurs when not enough melanin is produced to protect the skin.*

WHAT MAKES HAIR CURL?

▶ *Whether hair curls depends on the kind of follicle from which it grows. Round follicles produce straight hair, oval ones wavy hair and flat follicles curly hair.*

● Round follicle   ━ Oval follicle   Flat follicle

Skin and Hair

Skin is very important for a number of reasons. It protects all the different internal parts of the body from the outside world, and helps to prevent harmful germs from entering it (see page 41). Skin helps to control the body's internal temperature (see page 25), and it acts like a waterproof coat which keeps water in the body from evaporating. It is also extremely sensitive to touch, heat, cold and pain.

Skin and color

One of the skin's most important functions is to shield the body from the harmful ultraviolet rays of the sun. It does this with a substance called *melanin*. The more melanin your skin contains, the darker it is. The only reason why some people are black, some brown and some white is that, thousands of years ago, their ancestors came from hotter or colder parts of the world. Skin color is passed by the genes from parent to child (see page 30) and so cannot be altered.

Layers of the skin

The skin has two layers. The outer layer, the epidermis, consists of dead cells made of a tough substance called *keratin*. They flake off continuously and are replaced by new cells made by the malpighian layer. The second layer, the dermis, contains blood vessels, nerve endings and sweat glands. The skin itches when the nerve endings for pain in the epidermis are stimulated slightly (see page 57).

Hair

Hair is a special kind of covering. Like skin, it protects the body. And like skin too, hairs are made of dead cells of keratin. They grow out of small pits in the skin called follicles. Most people have about 100,000 hairs on their head. They lose between 30 and 60 a day as the follicles attached to them wither. The follicles then rest for 3 to 4 months before they grow new hair. The whole cycle lasts between one and six years. Most hairs can grow to between 600 and 750 mm (24–30 in.) long.

Hair on the scalp grows at a rate of about 0.33 mm (0.01 in.) a day, which means that it takes about six years to grow hair long enough to sit on.

Nails

Nails are also made of keratin. Their main purpose is to protect the ends of the fingers and toes, though, like a cat's claws, they are sometimes used for fighting!

Moles occur when the cells which contain melanin group together unevenly.

Freckles are caused by an uneven distribution of melanin throughout the skin.

Warts are small rough tumors on the skin. They are harmless but infectious. Verrucas, found on the sole of the foot, are similar to warts, but grow inward.

11

Bones and Joints

Adults have about 206 bones. Together these are called the skeleton. The skeleton is a kind of container, or framework, for the internal organs. It gives the body its shape and strength. It also supports it. When you jump from a height, the bones absorb the shock as you hit the ground. The skeleton also gives special protection to different parts of the body. The rib cage, for instance, surrounds the heart and lungs, and the backbone encloses the nerves leading down from the brain through the spinal column.

Bones may seem to be dry and lifeless. In fact they store important minerals, such as calcium, that the body needs. Bones are filled with a fatty material called bone, or white, marrow. Red and white blood cells are manufactured in the marrow and sent out into the bloodstream.

Babies' bones are made of rubbery material called cartilage. They go on growing throughout childhood and take about 25 years to ossify, or harden completely. Even so, most bones have a capping of cartilage left at the end, which acts as a shock absorber. If a bone is broken, the two ends slowly grow together again. A broken bone may be cased in plaster to make sure that the bone heals straight. Cartilage mends faster than bone, which is why children recover from broken bones sooner than adults.

Moving around

Bones are pulled by muscles. Without muscles we would be unable to move.

The place where two or more bones meet is called a joint. There are several types of joint. They allow different parts of our bodies to move in different ways. Joints are held together by strong tissues called ligaments which stop the muscles moving the bones too far. A special fluid which oils the joints and the cartilage at the ends of the bones, help the bones to move smoothly.

INSIDE THE ELBOW

▼ *Where two bones meet, a joint is formed. To prevent bones in a joint rubbing against each other, they are covered with tough cartilage which is slippery and smooth. Cartilage and synovial fluid together allow friction-free movement. Bones in a joint are held together by ligaments which prevent bones moving out of position.*

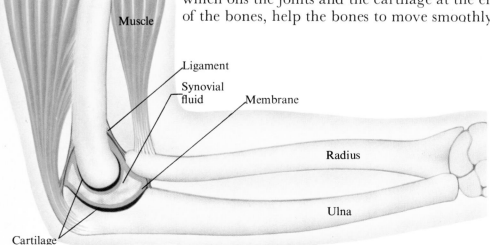

Muscle

Ligament

Synovial fluid

Membrane

Radius

Ulna

Cartilage

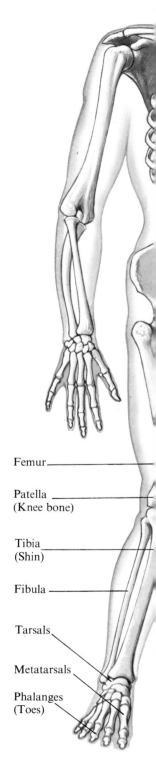

Femur

Patella (Knee bone)

Tibia (Shin)

Fibula

Tarsals

Metatarsals

Phalanges (Toes)

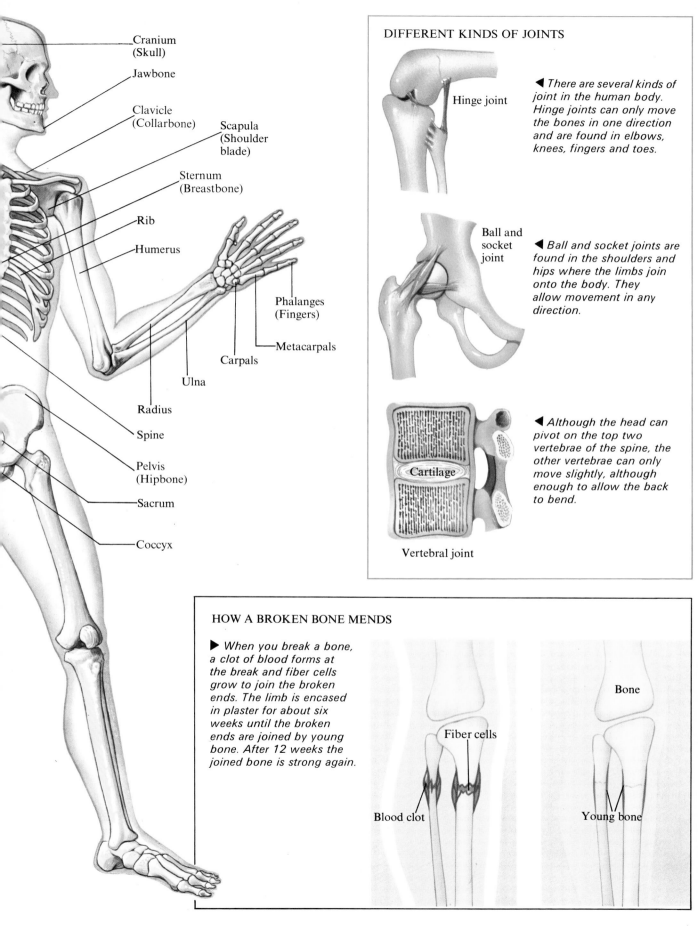

Cranium
(Skull)

Jawbone

Clavicle
(Collarbone)

Scapula
(Shoulder
blade)

Sternum
(Breastbone)

Rib

Humerus

Phalanges
(Fingers)

Metacarpals

Carpals

Ulna

Radius

Spine

Pelvis
(Hipbone)

Sacrum

Coccyx

DIFFERENT KINDS OF JOINTS

Hinge joint

◄ *There are several kinds of joint in the human body. Hinge joints can only move the bones in one direction and are found in elbows, knees, fingers and toes.*

Ball and socket joint

◄ *Ball and socket joints are found in the shoulders and hips where the limbs join onto the body. They allow movement in any direction.*

Cartilage

◄ *Although the head can pivot on the top two vertebrae of the spine, the other vertebrae can only move slightly, although enough to allow the back to bend.*

Vertebral joint

HOW A BROKEN BONE MENDS

▶ *When you break a bone, a clot of blood forms at the break and fiber cells grow to join the broken ends. The limb is encased in plaster for about six weeks until the broken ends are joined by young bone. After 12 weeks the joined bone is strong again.*

Fiber cells

Bone

Blood clot

Young bone

Muscles and Move- ment

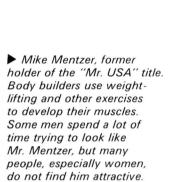

▶ *Mike Mentzer, former holder of the "Mr. USA" title. Body builders use weight-lifting and other exercises to develop their muscles. Some men spend a lot of time trying to look like Mr. Mentzer, but many people, especially women, do not find him attractive.*

HOW MUSCLES WORK

Muscles are made up of bundles of fibers. As the fibers contract, the muscle becomes shorter and thicker. The muscle fibers are made up of muscle cells

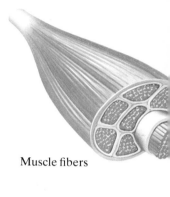

Muscle fibers

Every time we move, we use some of our muscles. Joints allow the bones to move, but muscles actually produce the movement.

There are about 656 muscles in the body. Each controls a particular movement. The thigh muscles, for instance, bend and straighten the knee. Others close and open the eyelids. Most movements make use of a large number of muscles. Over 200 are used every time you take one step.

Muscles can only pull. They never push. As a result they work in pairs. If you bend your knee, one muscle contracts—that is, it gets shorter and fatter—as it pulls the bone, while its partner relaxes. When you straighten your leg again, the reverse happens.

Muscles are attached to the bones by tendons. Some tendons are very long. The muscles that move your fingers are in your arm. You can feel the tendons in the back of your hand.

Muscles are made of bundles of fiber. The fibers are connected to the nervous system. Each fiber can contract when it receives a signal from the nerve. If we contracted all the fibers every time we moved a muscle, however, our movements would be very clumsy and imprecise. To stop this happening, some movements only contract some muscle fibers.

However much we use our muscles, the number of fibers they contain stays the same. But the fibers do become stronger and more powerful after regular exercise, and the muscles can also go on working longer without getting tired. Regular exercise helps to stop our muscles getting slack and stiff. Sportsmen develop the muscles in the parts of the body they use most. Cyclists and football players, for instance, develop very powerful leg muscles.

Muscles get their energy from food and oxygen supplied by the blood. The harder they work, the more energy they need and the more heat they create. Running fast makes you pant, which means that your lungs take in more oxygen. Your heart also starts to beat faster, so that the blood reaches your muscles more rapidly.

As the muscles burn up energy, a waste product called lactic acid collects in them. This makes them ache until it is carried away by the blood.

Involuntary muscles

Many of the body's muscles are called voluntary muscles because we can control them. Some are known as involuntary muscles. They work automatically and operate such things as the digestive system, the heart and part of the circulatory system.

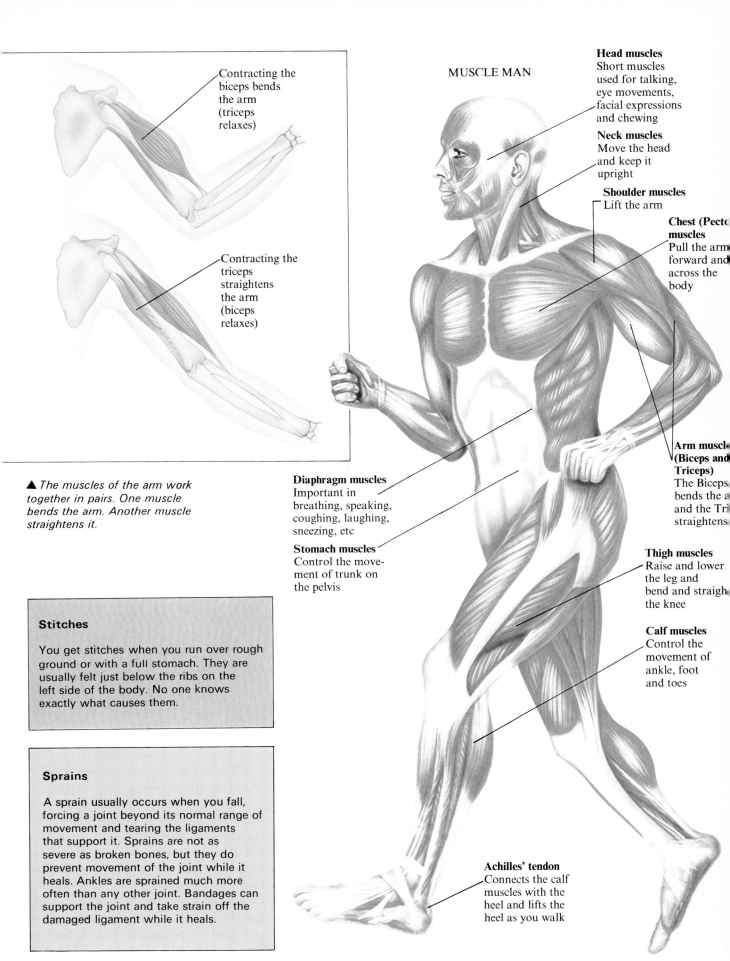

Contracting the biceps bends the arm (triceps relaxes)

Contracting the triceps straightens the arm (biceps relaxes)

▲ *The muscles of the arm work together in pairs. One muscle bends the arm. Another muscle straightens it.*

MUSCLE MAN

Head muscles
Short muscles used for talking, eye movements, facial expressions and chewing

Neck muscles
Move the head and keep it upright

Shoulder muscles
Lift the arm

Chest (Pecto muscles
Pull the arm forward and across the body

Arm muscle (Biceps and Triceps)
The Biceps bends the a and the Tri straightens

Thigh muscles
Raise and lower the leg and bend and straigh the knee

Calf muscles
Control the movement of ankle, foot and toes

Diaphragm muscles
Important in breathing, speaking, coughing, laughing, sneezing, etc

Stomach muscles
Control the movement of trunk on the pelvis

Achilles' tendon
Connects the calf muscles with the heel and lifts the heel as you walk

Stitches

You get stitches when you run over rough ground or with a full stomach. They are usually felt just below the ribs on the left side of the body. No one knows exactly what causes them.

Sprains

A sprain usually occurs when you fall, forcing a joint beyond its normal range of movement and tearing the ligaments that support it. Sprains are not as severe as broken bones, but they do prevent movement of the joint while it heals. Ankles are sprained much more often than any other joint. Bandages can support the joint and take strain off the damaged ligament while it heals.

Chapter Two

Inside the Body

▲ *Eating a watermelon is the first stage in its long journey through the digestive system to supply the body with energy and help to renew its cells.*

Our insides are an incredibly complicated machine, far more complex than anything man has ever made. Everyone's machine works in the same way. Whatever we look like outside, however much one individual is different from another, we are all the same inside. There are, of course, some physical differences between men and women (see chapter 3).

This amazing machine works from the moment we are born until we die. Some parts start working before we are born, and our hair goes on growing for a few days after the heart has stopped beating.

What does this machine do? The short answer is everything we need it to do to live. It takes in oxygen and distributes it around the body via the blood. It processes the food we eat, breaking it down in the digestive system and sending it, via the bloodstream,

to the different parts of the body that need it. It adjusts to the climate outside so that its internal temperature is normally exactly what it should be. It even has a very efficient waste-disposal system. Wastes from the body are absorbed into the blood which is purified as it passes through the kidneys.

But the biggest advantage that our body machine has over man-made machines is that almost everything happens automatically, without our having to control it. Whatever we are doing, our heart goes on beating, food is digested, blood circulates. In fact, we usually only need to think about what is happening in our bodies when something goes wrong with them.

▶ *A baby's blood vessels. The circulatory system is made up of veins and arteries. Arteries carry oxygenated blood to all parts of the body. Veins take blood back from the body to the heart and then to the lungs.*

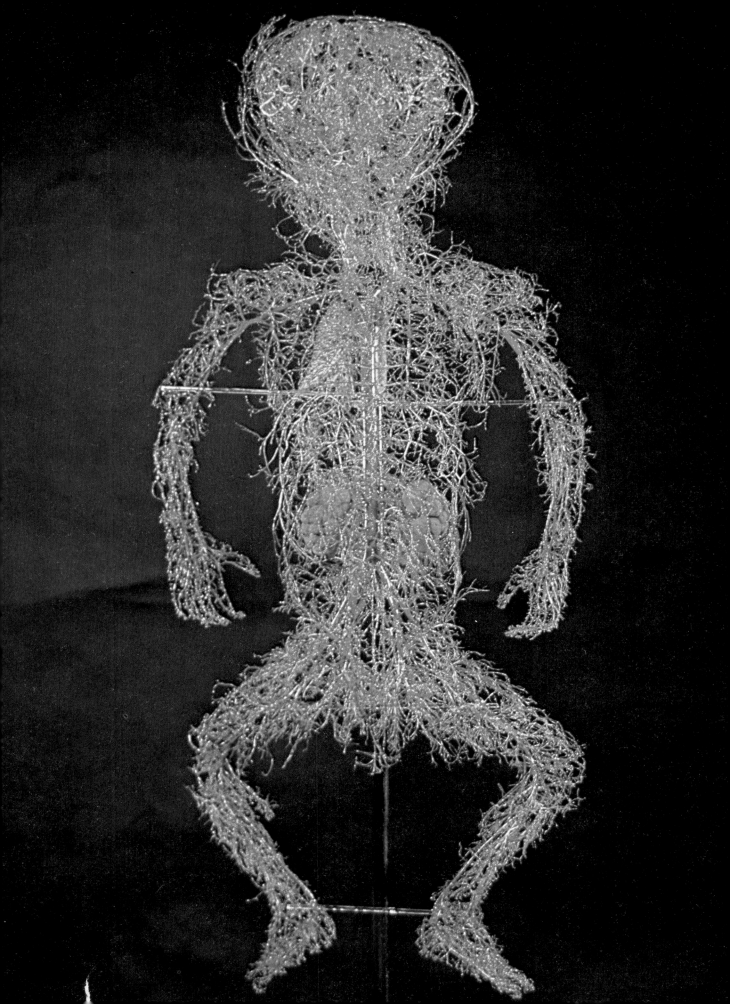

The Fate of Food

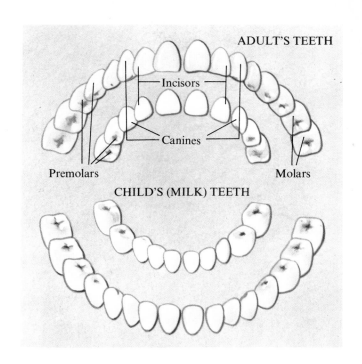

ADULT'S TEETH

Incisors

Canines

Premolars

Molars

CHILD'S (MILK) TEETH

Food provides the body with two essentials: the energy it needs to continue to function and the raw materials it needs to build new cells.

Balanced diets

Different kinds of foods do different jobs. Proteins —meat, fish, eggs, milk, cheese, beans—build the body up and renew its cells; carbohydrates— bread, sugar, potatoes—and fats—milk, eggs, butter and margarine and animal fats—supply energy.

Eating the right amount of the right foods is very important for keeping healthy. There is more information about this in chapter 4.

Digestion

Before it can start to do its work, all food, whether protein, carbohydrate or fat, has to be digested. That is, it has to be broken down chemically into small enough molecules to pass into the blood which takes it to all the different cells in the body.

Eating a mouthful of food is just the first stage of a long journey. As you chew, your teeth cut up the food into small pieces, which are softened by saliva and formed into a ball. When you swallow, the ball starts down the gullet towards the stomach.

If the stomach didn't exist, we would have to eat a little food about every 30 minutes to keep our bodies supplied with enough energy. The stomach stores food for about two to four hours, continuing to break it down. Gastric juices assist the process, and slowly the whole mixture turns into a creamy soup called *chyme*.

The next stage is the last and most important. The chyme moves in slow spurts from the stomach into the small intestine. There it is broken down into tiny particles by bile and other gastric juices. Then it flows forward over millions of tiny villi sticking out into the intestine. These absorb all the useful parts of the food into the blood-stream and the lymphatic system.

The leftovers—which consist of water and waste without value to the body—then pass slowly through the large intestine. From there, most of the water returns to the bloodstream, and the waste gradually gets harder, forming *feces*. These move into the rectum and leave the body through the anus when you go to the lavatory.

▲ *A baby is normally born with no teeth at all although by the time it is two it has grown all 20 milk teeth. These fall out as their roots dissolve, and are replaced after the age of five by 32 permanent teeth. These may not all appear until the age of 17 or more.*

THE DIGESTIVE SYSTEM

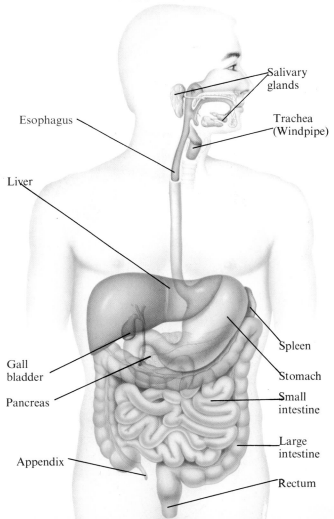

Salivary glands

Trachea (Windpipe)

Esophagus

Liver

Spleen

Gall bladder

Stomach

Pancreas

Small intestine

Large intestine

Appendix

Rectum

WHAT HAPPENS WHEN YOU EAT

Choking
Normally, when you swallow, the epiglottis closes over the windpipe to prevent food and drink going down the wrong way. Occasionally the epiglottis fails to cover the windpipe properly and food gets stuck in the top of the windpipe. Choking helps to clear it.

IN THE MOUTH

Front teeth bite off food

Molars break food down

Tongue moves food around mouth

Saliva helps to break food down

Epiglottis stops food going into windpipe

Food moves out of mouth down throat

Vomiting
Vomiting is a reflex action caused by eating too much or by an invasion of the stomach by bacteria. The abdominal wall and the diaphragm contract squeezing the stomach. The passageway to the small intestine closes, so that the contents of the stomach are forced upward.

Indigestion
Indigestion usually occurs when something goes wrong with the digestive system in the stomach. The usual causes are overeating, eating too fast, bad diet and heavy smoking.

IN THE STOMACH

Digestive juices in

A tight circular sphincter muscle allows the soup to move slowly into the small intestine

Some sugar moves into blood

The stomach squeezes and moves all the time. Gastric juices mix with the food. It is slowly broken down and forms a kind of soup

Stomach ulcers
Sometimes excess acid in the stomach wears away a small patch in the lining, forming an ulcer. This may be caused by worry, anxiety or perhaps by eating irregularly. Stomach ulcers are very painful. They are treated with rest, drugs and special diet.

Food stays in the stomach for 4–6 hours

Food stays in small intestine for up to 5 hours

Digestive juices in

IN THE SMALL INTESTINE
Bile and other juices mix with the soup. Fats, sugars, proteins, vitamins (useful parts of food) are now small enough to move into the blood

Diarrhea
Diarrhea is caused by bacteria or viruses invading the body and inflaming the intestine. Waste matter then passes too quickly through the large intestine which does not have time to drain off the water from it. The water waste then moves into the rectum and is expelled through the anus.

Useful food out to blood

Water and rest of food (waste) moves to large intestine

The Appendix
The appendix is an obscure part of the large intestine between 50 and 150 mm (2–6 in.) long. It is thought that millions of years ago it did have some useful purpose. Appendicitis—inflammation of the appendix—is still one of the commonest illnesses.

IN THE LARGE INTESTINE

Water moves into blood

Waste food forms a sludgy solid

When waste is ready to leave the body it moves into the rectum and then out through the anus when you go to the lavatory

Blood and the Heart

▶ *The heart pumps blood around the body. The entire blood supply passes through the heart from the lungs, which supply the blood with oxygen, before being pumped to the rest of the body. It returns to the heart from the body before going to the lungs to collect oxygen.*

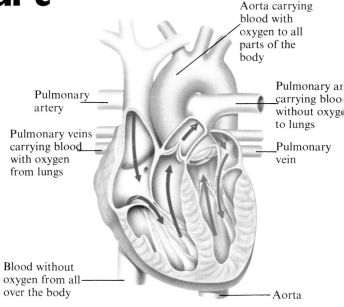

Aorta carrying blood with oxygen to all parts of the body

Pulmonary artery

Pulmonary artery carrying blood without oxygen to lungs

Pulmonary veins carrying blood with oxygen from lungs

Pulmonary vein

Blood without oxygen from all over the body

Aorta

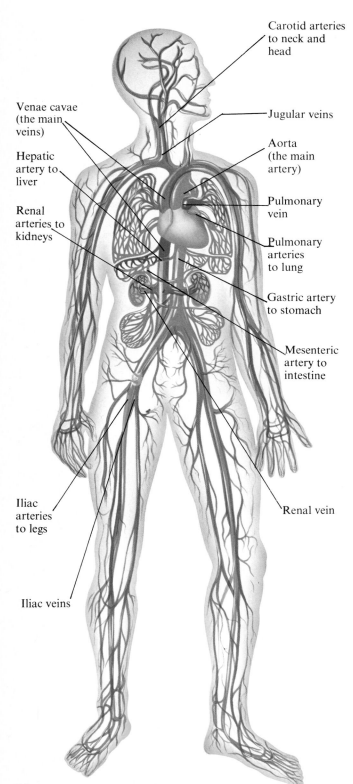

Carotid arteries to neck and head

Venae cavae (the main veins)

Hepatic artery to liver

Renal arteries to kidneys

Jugular veins

Aorta (the main artery)

Pulmonary vein

Pulmonary arteries to lung

Gastric artery to stomach

Mesenteric artery to intestine

Renal vein

Iliac arteries to legs

Iliac veins

Blood travels to every part of the body. It brings food and oxygen and takes away some of the body's waste products. It also spreads heat from the muscles and liver to the rest of the body.

The circulatory system

The heart pumps the blood. Each drop of blood does not go all the way around the body. Some of it goes from the heart to the brain, some to the muscles, or to the skin and skeleton, and a little stays within the heart itself.

The blood leaves from the left side of the heart. First of all it travels along arteries which gradually divide into thousands of tiny capillaries. In the capillaries the blood exchanges its food and

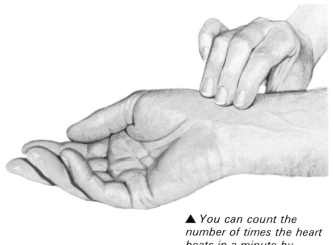

▲ *You can count the number of times the heart beats in a minute by counting the pulse beats in the wrist.*

oxygen for waste carbon dioxide from the cells. Then it travels along veins back to the right side of the heart.

The last stage of the journey is to the lungs. There the blood gets rid of waste carbon dioxide and collects its oxygen supply. Then it returns to the left side of the heart. Blood that contains oxygen is bright red. It gets darker as it flows around the body and loses its oxygen.

The arteries, capillaries and veins are called the circulatory system. Together they measure over 100,000 km (62,500 miles) and could stretch eight times around the world at the equator.

Because arteries carry blood away from the heart, they have thicker walls than veins. This is to stand up to the surge of high pressure caused by the heartbeat.

Blood does not always circulate evenly. When we run very fast, for instance, the muscles get much more than usual, and some other parts get

less. Without blood, living tissue would soon rot and die. The brain is permanently damaged if it is deprived of the blood's oxygen for only four minutes, but most other parts of the body can survive for longer without blood.

Blood groups

Adult men have 5 to 6 litres (10 to 12 pints) of blood. Women have about a litre (2 pints) less. Everyone's blood belongs to one of four main groups. These are called A, B, AB and O.

If you lose a lot of blood, you may have to be given a blood transfusion. This means that someone else's blood is fed into your veins. The new blood has to be able to mix with your own. If you have group AB blood, you can receive blood from all other groups. If you have Group O blood, however, you can only receive Group O, though you can give blood to all other groups. Before you receive a transfusion, your blood has to be tested.

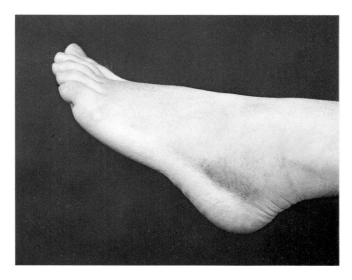

▲ A bruised foot, caused perhaps by a wrench or by something heavy dropping on it. Bruising occurs when there is bleeding beneath the skin but the skin itself is not broken. Bruises turn from black to purple to yellow as they heal.

Blood pressure and nosebleeds

Blood is pumped around the body under pressure. The pressure normally increases when your heart beats faster or when you are afraid or nervous.

Continual high blood pressure can be very serious. The arteries thicken to withstand the pressure, gradually restricting the flow of blood. Untreated, high blood pressure can cause a heart attack.

Nosebleeds may be the result of high blood pressure but are usually much less serious. They are often caused by the accidental injury of an exposed vein.

HOW A WOUND HEALS

As blood flows through an open wound, it tends to thicken and clot. It forms a delicate web which traps blood cells.

The trapped blood cells dry and shrink to form a scab over the web. The scab stops dirt getting into the wound.

New skin grows beneath the scab. When it is fully formed, the scab falls off.

Breathing and Talking

When we breathe in, we draw oxygen from the atmosphere into our lungs. When, a moment later, we breathe out, waste carbon dioxide from the body is expelled into the atmosphere.

Air travels up the nostrils, then through the pharynx and down the trachea, or windpipe, to the bronchi. One bronchus leads to the left lung, the other to the right one. The two bronchi eventually divide up into about 300 million tiny alveoli. These allow oxygen to pass into the bloodstream and take the carbon dioxide from it.

When we breathe out, the air containing the carbon dioxide travels by the same route.

The air we breathe is dirty and full of particles that are harmful to the body. So before it reaches the lungs it has to be cleaned. All the passages it travels along are lined with tiny hair-like cilia that catch the dirt and sweep it onto damp mucus. Blowing your nose gets rid of the mucus from the nostrils, which also contain big hairs to catch the larger bits of dirt. This is why it is important to breathe in through the nose rather than the mouth.

Too much carbon dioxide poisons the body. Try holding your breath. After about three quarters of a minute, often much less, you automatically start to breathe again. This is because too much carbon dioxide has built up inside your body. Air we breathe in contains about 0.03% carbon dioxide; air we breathe out contains about 4%.

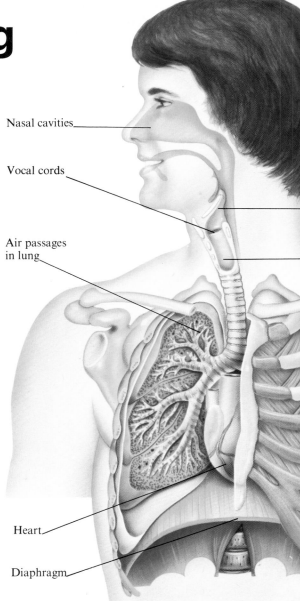

Nasal cavities

Vocal cords

Air passages in lung

Heart

Diaphragm

BREATHING IN

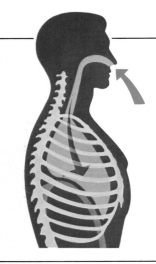

◀ When you breathe in, the rib muscles and diaphragm contract, so leaving more space in the chest for the air.

▶ When you breathe out, the rib muscles and diaphragm relax, so pushing air out of the lungs.

BREATHING OUT

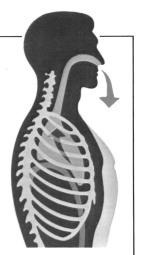

Sore Throat

A sore throat is caused by invading germs. The part affected is the middle of the pharynx. If the infection is particularly bad, it may spread down to the voice box, making your voice hoarse.

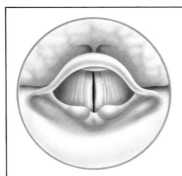
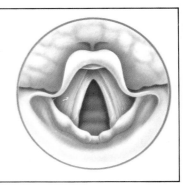

THE VOICE BOX

The larynx consists of two bands of cartilage with a small gap between them. These bands are the vocal cords. Air passing through the gap produces sound.

◀ A cutaway view to show how you breathe. Air flows down the trachea to the lungs, which are protected by the rib muscles and the diaphragm.

—— Epiglottis

Windpipe
—— (Trachea)

╲ Ribs

╲ Rib
muscles

As we breathe out, the air coming up from the lungs passes through the larynx, or voice box, which is at the top of the trachea. The larynx contains the vocal cords. When these vibrate as the air passes through, sounds are produced.

Making sounds is not the same as speaking. You can speak to yourself without making a noise. And although babies can make sounds, they are not able to speak. But no matter which language their parents speak, all babies make virtually the same sounds.

Learning to articulate—that is, to form recognizable sounds—means learning how to control the lips, jaw, teeth, tongue and palate (the roof of the mouth). Every word you say is formed by some or all of these working with the sounds produced by the vocal cords. The picture on the right shows that for one short word, "Julia", three different combinations have to be formed.

Some sounds have to be learned and take longer to master than others. Many children are six or seven before they can pronounce the "th" sounds in words such as "father" and "think". Nevertheless, it is always easier to learn new sounds and languages when you are young.

Loudness and pitch

How loud we talk depends on how hard we breathe out. We can go on talking without stopping for breath for much longer than we can shout.

Pitch depends on how long the vocal cords are and also on how tight they are. Men's voices get deeper, or break, when their vocal cords grow longer than women's. This usually happens between the ages of 13 and 16, although the cords of both sexes go on growing until about the age of 30.

We get hiccups when we breathe in irregularly. They occur when a nerve supplying the diaphragm suddenly closes, causing cramp-like contractions.

JULIA

Joo-

-lee-

-ah

Coughing

You cough when something, such as smoke or mucus, irritates the throat or bronchial passages, or when they have been inflamed by germs. You try to breathe out while your vocal cords are closed. This raises the pressure of the air, which explodes out when the cords finally open, helping to clear the passages.

Sneezing

You may sneeze when something, such as dust or pollen irritates the nasal passages. The glottis—the gap between the vocal cords—stays open all the time. The tongue rises up to block the mouth, so that the air and mucus rush out through the nose, helping to clear it.

Losing Water

▶ *About two thirds of our bodies consist of water, which is far more vital to survival than food. We can do without food for more than two months but without water for only a few days.*

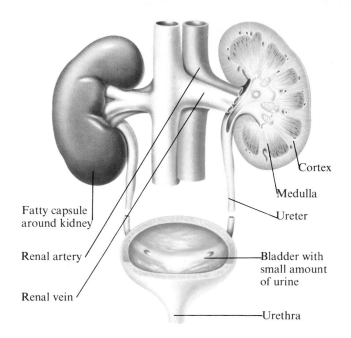

Cortex

Medulla

Ureter

Fatty capsule around kidney

Renal artery

Bladder with small amount of urine

Renal vein

Urethra

▲ *The kidneys extract all the body's waste products from the blood and get rid of them in the form of urine. Urine drips down the ureters from the kidneys into the bladder.*

Man is a watery animal. About two thirds of the body consists of water. Most of it is contained within the cells, but about a quarter surrounds the tissues or forms part of the blood.

The water balance

Keeping the right amount of water in our bodies is extremely important. With too little we become dehydrated and eventually die. Feeling thirsty is a sign that our bodies have too little water.

Any kind of activity makes us lose water. How much we lose varies a great deal and depends on climate and the sort of work we do. The average loss is about 2 to 3 litres (4 to 6 pints) a day. About half of this is replaced by drinking. The other half comes from the food we eat (potatoes, for instance, are 75% water, cheese 28%).

The body loses water in several different ways. It goes out through the lungs when we breathe and also through the skin. A little goes out with the feces. This only represents about half of the water we need to lose every day, however. The rest leaves our bodies in the form of urine.

The kidneys

Urine is made in the kidneys. These are a complicated filter system, made up of millions of tiny blood vessels. As all the blood from the body passes through them, they extract the waste products the body no longer needs. About 96% of urine is water. The rest is urea and other salts.

Urea is the waste from the protein we eat and gives the urine its yellow color. The kidneys respond to the body's needs and can vary the amount of water they take from the blood. Usually, though, it is about one percent of the total water in the body.

The urine moves from the kidneys down the ureters to the bladder. A sphincter muscle around the outlet of the bladder prevents the urine from escaping. When the bladder is nearly full, we feel the need to urinate. When we do so, urine passes down the urethra.

KEEPING COOL

▶ *This hot and sweating man may long for a cool shower but already his body is cooling itself down. The sweat evaporates in the air. His face is red because more blood is flowing near the surface and so is being cooled. A cool drink, however, will help to replace the water lost in sweating.*

Not too Hot, Not too Cold

No matter how hot or cold it is outside, the temperature inside the body stays about the same. If the body had not developed many ways of keeping its internal temperature constant, it would be impossible to live in very hot or cold areas.

Much of the food we eat is used for keeping us warm. Heat is made by the muscles and spread around the body by the blood.

Keeping cool

When it gets hot outside, or if we make too much heat energy, the blood vessels in the skin get wider, so that more blood reaches the skin. As a result, more heat is lost. We also start to sweat, and as the sweat evaporates it cools us down.

Keeping hot

When it gets cold the blood vessels in the dermis get smaller and so less heat is lost through the skin. Shivering warms us up too, since the tiny movements of our muscles produce heat.

In extreme cold, the furthest tips of the body— nose, fingers, toes—may suffer from frostbite. This happens when blood fails to reach them and their food and oxygen supply is cut off. As a result, waste products begin to build up, and the affected area starts to rot.

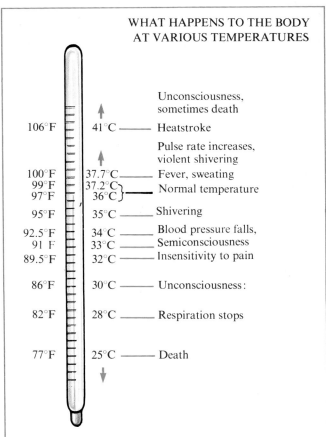

WHAT HAPPENS TO THE BODY
AT VARIOUS TEMPERATURES

°F	°C	
		Unconsciousness, sometimes death
106°F	41°C	Heatstroke
		Pulse rate increases, violent shivering
100°F	37.7°C	Fever, sweating
99°F	37.2°C	Normal temperature
97°F	36°C	
95°F	35°C	Shivering
92.5°F	34°C	Blood pressure falls,
91 F	33°C	Semiconsciousness
89.5°F	32°C	Insensitivity to pain
86°F	30°C	Unconsciousness:
82°F	28°C	Respiration stops
77°F	25°C	Death

▲ The body has many mechanisms for keeping its internal temperature constant. Sometimes, though, when the weather is either very hot or very cold, these mechanisms break down. This is what happens to the body when they do.

Goose pimples

KEEPING WARM

▶ This girl is shivering, which automatically helps to keep the body warm in cold weather. The tiny movements of her muscles help to warm the body. In addition, goose pimples make body hairs stand on end, so trapping warm air between them.

Normal body temperature
The usual body temperature for most people is 36.8° to 37.0°C (98.6°F). It often varies however—even the time of day makes a difference—and a higher or lower figure is not necessarily a sign of illness.

▲ Old age comes toward the end of the cycle of life, which begins with conception and birth and includes growing up, becoming adult and possibly having children of your own.

Chapter Three

A Lifetime

A child is created by its parents. Their genes decide its major characteristics, which it cannot change. For the first years of its life, it depends entirely on them for food and warmth, and for many years after that they play an extremely important part in its life.

Yet a baby is not an exact copy of its parents. Even in the first moments of its life it is a different person, who reacts to things in its own way. It soon develops its own personality. This depends on the people it meets, on the way it is brought up, in fact on everything that happens to it.

In fact, we never stop changing, both mentally and physically, throughout our lives. Mentally, we constantly react to new experiences—events, ideas, people. Our behavior and attitudes when we are 70 may be quite different from when we were 20.

Physically, our bodies are changing all the time too. At some periods, the change is faster than at others. At puberty, for instance, we not only grow taller and stronger (people call it "filling out"). Our reproductive system also develops, so that we are able to have children ourselves and start the process of human life all over again.

Later still, our bodies slowly begin to wear out, and we no longer function as well as we used to. Some people find this hard to accept, others easy, perhaps because they discover that what they have learned in life makes up for their physical decline. Finally though, something seizes up, and our heart and brain stop working and we die.

◀ A Japanese baby traveling in style on its mother's back. Babies are often in close contact with their mothers and a strong bond forms between them.

A New Life Begins

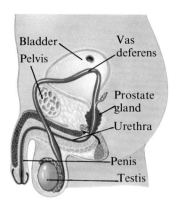

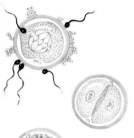

◀ The fertilized egg divides into two cells 30 hours after conception, and then continues to divide. The cells form different parts of the fetus.

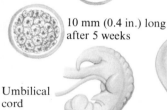

10 mm (0.4 in.) long after 5 weeks

Umbilical cord

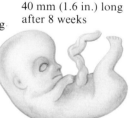

40 mm (1.6 in.) long after 8 weeks

A new life is made by a man and woman together. During sexual intercourse, millions of tiny sperm are pushed through the man's erect penis into the woman's vagina. Some of these sperm penetrate the cervix and enter the uterus, or womb. An even smaller number, perhaps only a few hundred, manage to continue into the Fallopian tubes. Normally even these few survivors die quickly. The only exception is when they meet an egg.

Once a month, a woman's ovaries produce a single egg cell. It travels along the Fallopian tubes in the direction of the uterus. If no sperm are waiting, it dies within about 48 hours. If sperm are there, they attack the egg, until eventually one sperm may succeed in entering it. This is the moment of conception, at which a new life starts to grow.

Sexual intercourse only leads to conception when sperm and egg meet. Conception can be prevented in several different ways. One of the most popular is the contraceptive pill. This prevents eggs being made and released. Some people prefer sterilization. Neither contraceptives nor sterilization stop people having sexual intercourse. Some religions forbid contraception.

HOW A BABY GROWS INSIDE ITS MOTHER

▼ At 10 weeks it is still only about 21 grams (0.75 oz). It is about 6 cm (2.5 in.) long. Its head is far bigger than the rest of its body.

▼ At 22 weeks it weighs about 630 grams (22 oz) and can grip firmly with its hands. Its mother can feel it moving.

▼ At 34 weeks, it is about 2300 grams (81 oz). Babies born at this time usually survive without difficulty.

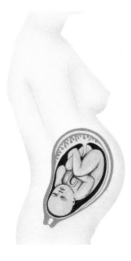

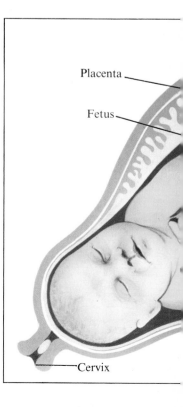

Placenta

Fetus

Cervix

Pregnancy

On average, there are 266 days between the moment of conception and the birth of a baby. This time can vary quite a lot from mother to mother, however.

The baby—or fetus, as it is called until it is born—develops very quickly in its mother's womb. Its heart starts to beat on the 25th day, and its circulatory system starts working on about the 49th day. By about the 84th day, all its major features are complete.

At this stage, however, the fetus is still tiny. It only weighs about 21 g (0.07 oz) and measures 70 mm (2.8 in.). For the rest of the time until it is born, it concentrates on growing, though refinements such as hair and nails only develop later. At birth, a baby weighs on average 3.29 kg (7.34 lb) and measures 508 mm (20 in.).

The fetus gets the food and oxygen it needs to grow and develop from its mother's bloodstream. The blood of mother and fetus do not mix, however. Instead, food and oxygen are passed to the fetus through the *placenta*. The fetal waste products are expelled through the placenta.

After about the 20th week, the fetus starts to suck its thumb, yawn, stretch and kick. From then until birth it grows about 50% longer. In the last few weeks before it is born, it turns so that its head is facing the cervix, the opening of the uterus into the vagina.

Birth

One of the first signs that the fetus is ready to be born is when the muscles of its mother's uterus start to contract. The contractions, which get longer and more frequent, open up the cervix to let the fetus pass through. Then the mother goes into labor. She uses all her strength to push the fetus through the cervix, along the vagina and out into the world. The baby is quickly followed by the placenta. The umbilical cord which joins the baby to the mother is cut by a midwife or a doctor.

The time a baby takes to be born varies enormously. Some mothers are in labor for only about two hours, others for 24 hours or even longer.

Most difficulties during birth occur because the fetus is facing the wrong way. In these cases, doctors can open the mother's womb and lift the baby out. This is called a Caesarian section.

Babies often arrive days or even weeks late or early. This does not matter, though if a baby is born very early it has to have special treatment in an incubator in the intensive care department of a hospital.

Most mothers nowadays have their babies in the hospital because of the special care which hospitals can provide for the mother and her child. Some women, though, prefer to have their babies at home in familiar surroundings.

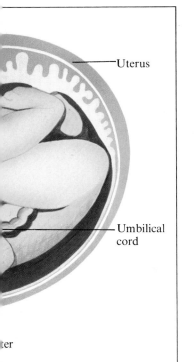

—Uterus

—Umbilical cord

er

◀ *A fully grown fetus inside its mother's womb. The umbilical cord joins the fetus to the placenta, and passes nourishment to it.*

▼*After about nine months, the baby's body has developed enough for it to survive outside the womb. One of the first signs that it is about to be born is the breaking of the water sac, often called the "breaking of the waters". The fluid escapes through the vagina.*

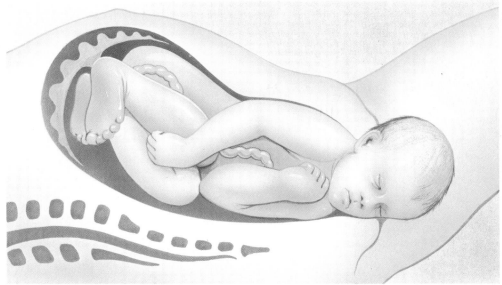

Who Do You Look Like?

WHAT MAKES YOU A GIRL OR A BOY?

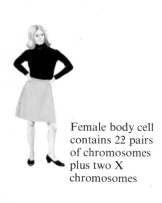

Female body cell contains 22 pairs of chromosomes plus two X chromosomes

Male body cell contains 22 pairs of chromosomes plus one X and one Y chromosome

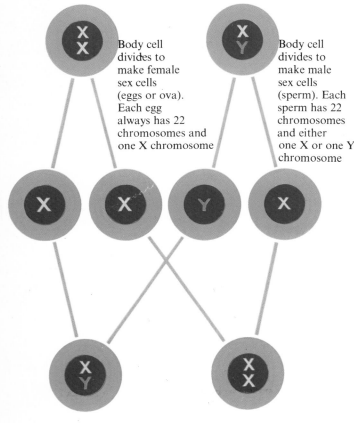

Body cell divides to make female sex cells (eggs or ova). Each egg always has 22 chromosomes and one X chromosome

Body cell divides to make male sex cells (sperm). Each sperm has 22 chromosomes and either one X or one Y chromosome

If a sperm with a Y chromosome fertilizes an egg, the fertilized egg will become a boy

If a sperm with an X chromosome fertilizes an egg, the fertilized egg will become a girl

Everyone inherits their basic physical characteristics through their parents' genes. These include such things as skin color, the shape of the face, eye color and blood group. Intelligence is also partly inherited.

Though we inherit these important characteristics from our parents, we do not grow up to be exact copies of them. All kinds of other things contribute to make us become unique individuals.

Chromosomes and genes

Every single cell in the human body except one contains 46 chromosomes. These are made up of

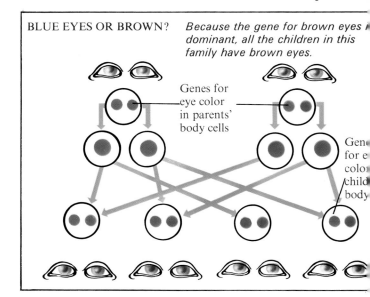

BLUE EYES OR BROWN? *Because the gene for brown eyes* *dominant, all the children in this* *family have brown eyes.*

Genes for eye color in parents' body cells

Gen for e colo child body

◀ *When several members of one family get together, it is easy to see in what ways they look alike.*

IDENTICAL TWINS
Identical twins occur when their mother's egg divides into two after it has been fertilized. The pattern of their genes is therefore exactly the same, and they inherit the same characteristics. Dissimilar twins are born when two different eggs are fertilized by two different sperm. They are often quite alike, just as brothers and sisters are, but they are not identical. Identical twins are always of the same sex. Dissimilar twins may both be male, both female, or one of each.

23 pairs. The exception is the sex cell, which has 23 single chromosomes. When the sperm and the egg fertilize, they each contribute 23 chromosomes, so that the fertilized egg has 46, exactly half from each parent.

Each chromosome contains hundreds of genes. Genes carry the information that decides our characteristics. We inherit one set of instructions for each characteristic from each of our parents. This means that we are not exactly identical to either of our parents.

Some genes are said to be dominant, others to be recessive. The combination of dominant and recessive genes that we inherit from our parents decides many of our characteristics. The diagram on inheriting eye color shows how different combinations can be passed on from parents to children. If one of a pair of genes is dominant, it will always prevail. Only if both genes are recessive will the recessive characteristic appear. As a result recessive characteristics, such as red hair, are sometimes hidden for several generations before they reappear.

Eye color is a very simple example of how inheritance works and the illustration below on the left shows how eye color is inherited. Most characteristics are decided by a number of genes, not just by one pair.

Chromosomes last for life. Their pattern cannot be changed. Some characteristics—baldness in men, for example—may not appear for a long time, however.

Boy or girl?

Two chromosomes govern which sex you are. They are called X and Y. Women have two X chromosomes. Men, however, have one X and one Y chromosome. Thus, a woman's egg always carries an X chromosome. A man's sperm carries an X or a Y. If it carries an X, the child's chromosomes will be XX, and she will be a girl. If the sperm carries a Y chromosome, the child's chromosomes will be XY, and he will be a boy.

Because both parents in this family have one gene for blue eyes, it is possible for some of their children to have blue eyes.

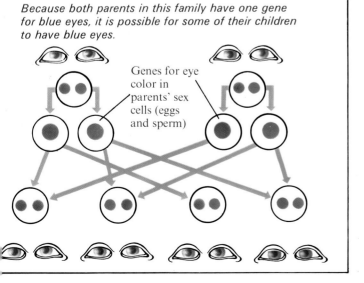

Genes for eye color in parents' sex cells (eggs and sperm)

Growing Up

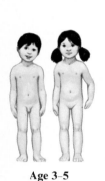 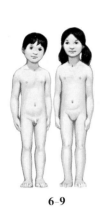 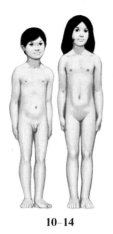 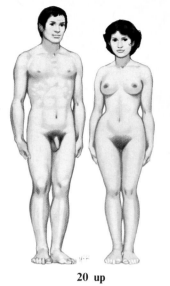

Age 3–5   **6–9**   **10–14**   **20 up**

▲ The body grows very rapidly during childhood and adolescence. Girls are usually fully grown at 17, boys at 18, though they may go on growing for a few more years.

Blushing
Blushing is a sign of embarrassment. The face becomes hot and red as the blood rushes to it. Young people often blush during puberty because they feel unsure of themselves, and are uncertain what to do.

▼ During puberty, a boy's body turns into a man's, a girl's into a woman's, and their reproductive systems begin to function.

The 38 weeks a fetus spends in its mother's womb are just the start of a far longer period of growth. During the next twenty years or so the child's body will grow and develop. Its understanding and intelligence will also develop, and it will adjust to living with other people.

Children do not grow at the same rate all the time. Nor do boys and girls always grow at the same pace. They grow quickly in the first few years, when they also learn to walk and talk (see pages 66–67). Another rapid change takes place in the period known as puberty.

Puberty

Puberty is the time when the reproductive system starts to work—that is, when boys begin to manufacture sperm and girls begin to menstruate, that is to produce the eggs that can be fertilized by sperm.

The age at which puberty begins varies enormously from person to person. The average starting age for girls is 11, for boys 12. These ages can vary a great deal in each direction. Puberty begins when the individual's body is ready for it, and an early or late start does not make any difference.

Puberty starts when the pituitary gland in the brain produces a new type of hormone (see page 58). These new hormones stimulate the ovaries in girls and the testes in boys to produce sex hormones. The sex hormones then set off a whole series of changes to the body which take several years to complete.

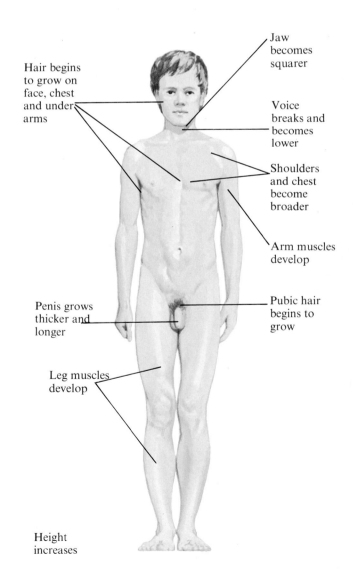

Hair begins to grow on face, chest and under arms

Jaw becomes squarer

Voice breaks and becomes lower

Shoulders and chest become broader

Arm muscles develop

Penis grows thicker and longer

Pubic hair begins to grow

Leg muscles develop

Height increases

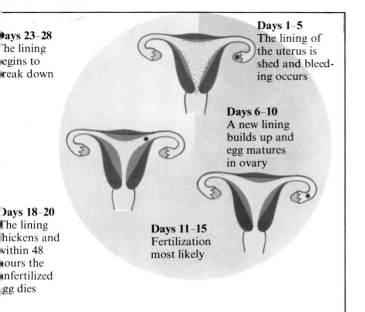

Days 23–28
The lining begins to break down

Days 1–5
The lining of the uterus is shed and bleeding occurs

Days 6–10
A new lining builds up and egg matures in ovary

Days 18–20
The lining thickens and within 48 hours the unfertilized egg dies

Days 11–15
Fertilization most likely

THE MENSTRUAL CYCLE

▲ Each month an egg leaves the ovaries and moves down the Fallopian tubes to the uterus. If the egg is not fertilized, the uterus' lining and egg leave the uterus during the period.

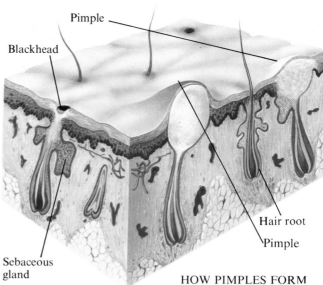

HOW PIMPLES FORM

Pimple
Blackhead
Hair root
Pimple
Sebaceous gland

▲ During puberty, blackheads and pimples often develop as the sebaceous glands get clogged with grease. Clean skin and medicated cream help to clear them up.

What happens in puberty

At puberty, boys suddenly start to grow much more quickly. The muscles develop, the penis gets larger, pubic hair starts to grow, as well as hair under the arms and on the face and body. The voice also breaks. Girls get much taller. In addition their breasts develop, their hips get wider, pubic hair and body hair begin to grow and they may gain a layer of fat.

All this means that at the end of puberty a girl's body has become that of a woman, a boy's that of a man. A girl can become pregnant, a boy can become a father.

Puberty and adolescence

Adolescence is the long and complicated period during which children slowly turn into adults. Puberty is the physical side of adolescence. The mental side, in which children become independent and look after themselves, takes far longer and finishes much later.

The menstrual cycle

The menstrual cycle begins when the ovaries begin to release an ovum each month. As the ovum travels down the oviduct, the uterus becomes ready to receive a fertilized egg. The lining of the uterus thickens, and the supply of blood to it increases. Usually the egg is not fertilized and the thickened lining breaks up and is released through the vagina. This menstrual bleeding is usually called a period, and is not always regular.

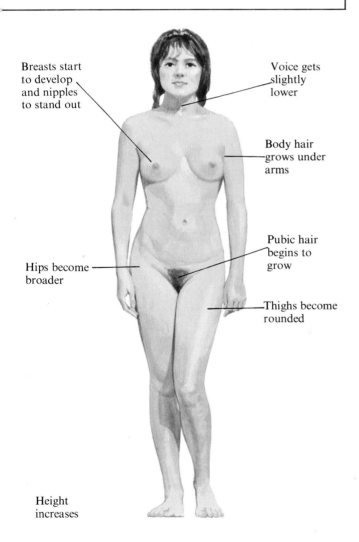

Breasts start to develop and nipples to stand out

Voice gets slightly lower

Body hair grows under arms

Hips become broader

Pubic hair begins to grow

Thighs become rounded

Height increases

Growing Old

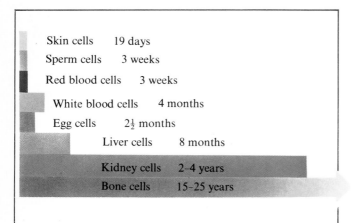

Skin cells	19 days	
Sperm cells	3 weeks	
Red blood cells	3 weeks	
White blood cells	4 months	
Egg cells	2½ months	
Liver cells	8 months	
Kidney cells	2–4 years	
Bone cells	15–25 years	

▲ Chart showing how long the cells that make up different parts of the body live. Most cells continually renew themselves, though in old age they do so more slowly.

Body cells
The human body is made up of an enormous number of individual cells, all of which are descendants of the fertilized egg produced at conception. It is to the cells that the blood carries food and oxygen. Each of them contains the genetic information that determines our physical characteristics.

The body's cells continually die and are replaced by new cells. Some cells—those of the intestine for instance—live for only a few days. Others last much longer. Those in the bones live for up to 30 years. The brain's cells cannot be renewed when they die.

SOME SIGNS OF OLD AGE

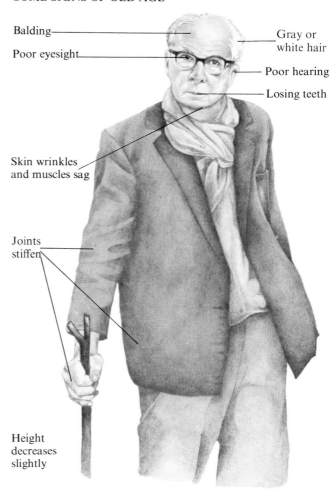

Balding

Gray or white hair

Poor eyesight

Poor hearing

Losing teeth

Skin wrinkles and muscles sag

Joints stiffen

Height decreases slightly

We start to grow old when we are about 25 or 30. This fact is not as frightening as it may seem. What it means is that the body is strongest and the brain most alert between the ages of 20 and 30. After that they slowly become less efficient, though the signs of old age do not become noticeable for many years. After they are about 50, women stop having periods and are unable to have children.

What happens in old age

As we get older, the cells of the body renew themselves more and more slowly. As a result, bones gradually become more brittle and break more easily. Muscles waste away and joints stiffen, so that movement becomes more difficult. Bones get smaller, and skin wrinkles, so that old people often become slightly shorter. At the same time, their senses begin to decline. Hearing and sight become worse, as do smell and taste.

Dead brain cells are not renewed at all. Therefore the brain slowly begins to work less efficiently the older we get. This means that memory can get poorer and thinking slower.

The consequence of all this is that old people are less able to resist disease. Their reactions are slower and they get more tired.

Ageing affects different people in different ways. Some people still seem to be quite young when they are 80, others quite old when they are 60. This may depend on their attitude to life and growing old.

Senility

Senility is the word used to describe a deterioration of the brain that sometimes happens when people grow old. Senile old people are often confused and forgetful and as a result cannot look after themselves. Only about 10% of old people ever suffer from senility.

Death

▲ The funeral of a British soldier killed in 1969. It is natural to feel grief when someone you know or love dies. Funerals are a way of expressing that grief in public. They can help you to accept that person's death.

When someone dies, he stops breathing. As a result, the supply of oxygen to the lungs ceases. If the heart stops pumping blood around the body, its cells receive no food and oxygen and die.

All this can happen, however, without a person necessarily being dead. The brain cells can survive for a few minutes without blood, the heart for 15 minutes, the kidneys for one hour and the rest of the body for a little longer still. Artificial respiration is one way of starting someone breathing again by breathing air into their lungs. So long as their cells have not been damaged, they will be perfectly all right. And in major operations doctors often use machines to keep their patients breathing or their blood circulating.

What really determines whether a person is dead or not is the activity in his brain. This can be measured by an EEG, or electro-encephalo-gram. The EEG records activity in the brain. If there is none, then the person is dead. In very doubtful cases, doctors let the EEG run for 24 hours without any signs of activity before they are prepared to declare someone dead.

Causes of death

You cannot die simply of old age. The heart does not stop beating and the brain working of their own accord. Something—a disease, an accident, a shock—has to make them stop.

The most common causes of death nowadays are strokes (when a blood clot interrupts the blood supply to part of the brain), heart failure and cancer. Until fairly recently, tuberculosis, and infectious diseases (see page 42) used to claim far more victims, and many more young children died.

Fainting

Fainting has nothing to do with dying. A person faints when the heart has not been able to pump enough blood to the brain. When you faint you collapse. This brings the brain to the same level as the heart and immediately restores the blood supply.

LIFE EXPECTANCIES THROUGH THE AGES	
18	Iron Age
28	A.D. 0
30	Rome, A.D. 600
35	England, 1250
30	England, 1550
34	England, 1700
39	England, 1815
49	England, 1900
60	England, 1940
71	England, 1961

Chapter Four

War Against Disease

DISORDERS AND DISEASES AFFECTING PARTICULAR PARTS OF THE BODY	
Nervous system	Polio, epilepsy, tetanus, rabies, encephalitis, meningitis, Parkinson's disease.
Respiratory system	Tuberculosis, bronchitis, asthma, pneumonia, laryngitis, pharyngitis.
Digestive system	Ulcers, food poisoning, cholera, typhoid, jaundice, hepatitis, parasites, appendicitis, gall stones.
Skin	Smallpox, measles, chicken pox, athlete's foot, impetigo, eczema, dermatitis, verrucas, warts, ringworm.
Excretory system	Cystitis, kidney stones, kidney failure.
Glands	Diabetes, goiter, mumps, gigantism, dwarfism.
Blood	Anemia, leukemia, hemophilia.
Arteries and Veins	Arteriosclerosis, varicose veins, piles.
Heart	Thrombosis, rheumatic fever.
Skeleton and muscles	Lumbago, sciatica, slipped disk, arthritis, muscular dystrophy.

Disease simply means "dis-ease". When we have a disease our body or mind is not at ease.

There are many different kinds of disease. We catch infectious diseases when tiny organisms called germs attack our bodies. Other types of disease are caused when part of our bodies begins to function badly or to break down. For instance, we may get arthritis when our joints begin to lose their protective cartilage or an ulcer if our digestive system starts to break down. There are also diseases of the mind. Only some of these have physical causes.

In the last fifty years or so, medicine has made enormous progress. All kinds of new methods of fighting, curing and preventing diseases have been discovered. Many illnesses that used to kill their victims can now be cured or prevented quite easily.

Illness still persists because, as some diseases have been conquered, others have taken their place. A century ago, infectious diseases were the big killers. In richer countries better living conditions and hygiene, helped by mass

▶ Doctors and nurses performing an operation in an Australian hospital. Operations can be a very dramatic way of treating a disease, and, if possible, doctors prefer to prevent people becoming ill at all.

immunization, have almost wiped out serious infectious diseases. In poorer countries, however, a lot of people still die from them.

Nowadays, far more people die from diseases such as cancer, strokes and heart attacks. These are not infectious diseases but are caused by such things as stress, smoking, too much rich food and too little exercise. They are all diseases brought about by the conditions of the busy modern world.

Our bodies have their own defenses against disease and start to fight invading germs automatically, without our knowing about it. In fact we only realize that we are ill when the battle is at its peak. The body's defenses can be helped by man-made drugs, which attack the invading germs. We can also resist disease much more effectively if we keep ourselves in good health by taking regular exercise and eating a proper diet.

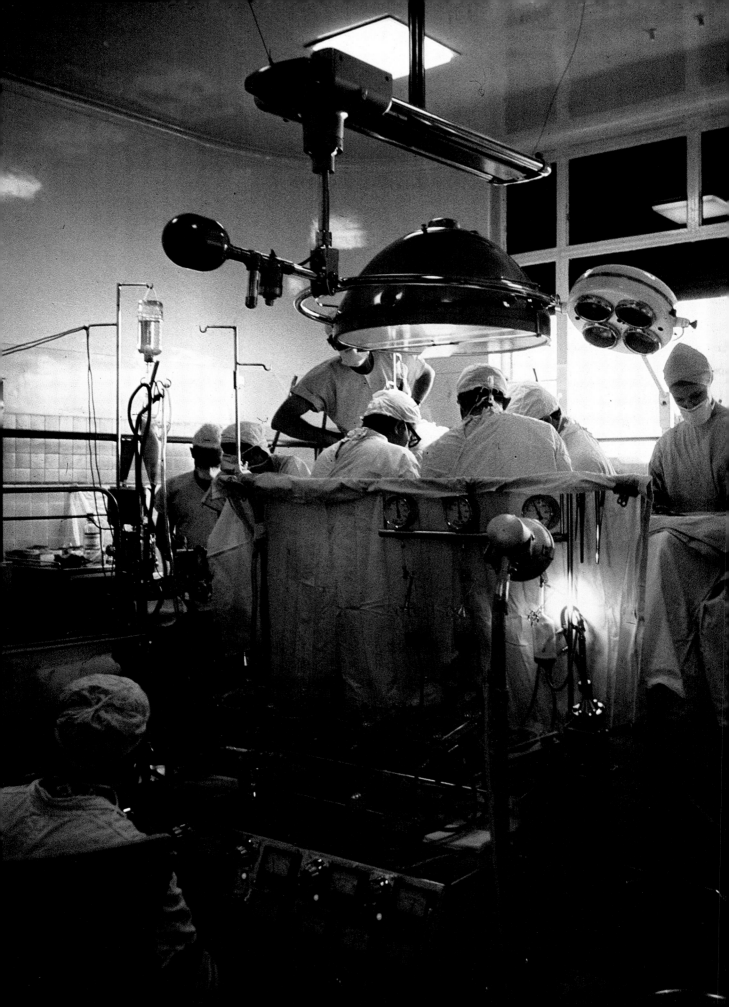

DIFFERENT KINDS OF FOOD

Some foods rich in protein

Some foods rich in carbohydrate

Some foods rich in vitamins and minerals

▶ These two boys from China are the same age. The one on the left is the average size for his age. His friend is smaller because his diet did not contain the right foods to ensure proper growth.

Keeping Healthy

Being healthy doesn't mean simply not being ill. Although we may not be suffering from a disease, we can do a lot to make sure that we are as healthy as possible.

Diet

The simplest and most important rule of diet is to eat sensibly, not too much or too little. Carbohydrates and fats may be the source of energy, but eating a lot of sugar or butter won't make you super-energetic. Once the body has absorbed all it needs, it simply stores the rest as fat. The same thing happens with proteins. Huge amounts of protein do not go on building you up so that you eventually become a superman. Instead, the liver breaks the excess down and uses it for energy or stores it as fat.

Our bodies also need tiny amounts of minerals and vitamins. Minerals help to build up the body, vitamins to change food into energy. We automatically get enough minerals and vitamins if the rest of our diet is properly balanced.

We also need to make sure that the food we eat contains enough roughage. This helps to get rid of waste food and is found in foods such as vegetables and wholemeal bread.

Every week, magazines and newspapers produce new ideas for losing weight. They all amount to the same thing, however—eating less. The best way to avoid having to diet is not to eat the wrong things in the first place.

Fresh air

Besides food, the body also needs oxygen, which we take from the air we breathe. Until quite recently, the air in most towns and cities was made filthy by the smoke of factory chimneys. This caused a lot of illness. Now, however, most Western countries have passed laws insisting on clean air.

Exercise

Taking exercise is another very important way of keeping healthy. A moderate amount of regular exercise helps to keep the body working efficiently. It strengthens the heart and muscles, improves the circulatory and respiratory systems and the posture of the body. All this makes you feel better and also improves your body's ability to fight disease. However, it does not help to reduce weight very much.

Occasional bouts of violent exercise are no good at all. In fact, they are harmful, since they put a sudden strain on the body. Most children, however, get all the exercise they need from their normal lives.

INSIDE A MOLAR TOOTH

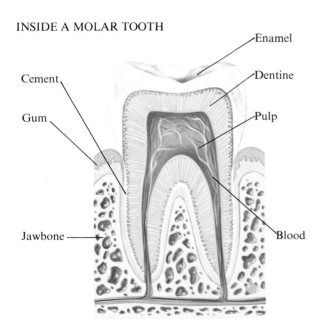

Enamel

Dentine

Cement

Pulp

Gum

Jawbone

Blood

▲ The molars are used for grinding food. The outer layer of enamel covers a layer of bone-like substance called dentine. Inside this is the pulp cavity which contains blood vessels and nerves.

▼ Central Park, New York, where many people keep fit by jogging and cycling. Jogging has become very popular recently, and people of all ages jog in the parks and city streets.

▼ Before a decaying tooth can be filled, the affected area has to be drilled away. Visiting the dentist regularly helps to stop tooth decay before it spreads too far.

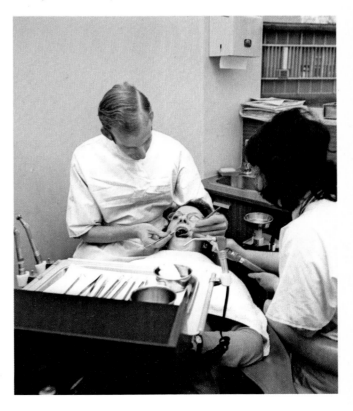

The Body's Defenses

The body has several lines of defense against invasion by germs and particles of dirt. The skin protects most of the body, unless it is cut or scratched. The eyes are particularly at risk. Eyelashes and eyelids help to keep dust out; eyelids and tears continually wash the eye. If something does get caught in the eye, extra tears help to wash it out.

Wax, saliva and different forms of mucus protect the other openings of the body. Tonsils, acid in the stomach and the digestive juices lie deeper in the body.

Should germs get through these defenses, and lodge in part of the body, white blood cells rush to attack them. White blood cells are made in the spleen and the lymph nodes.

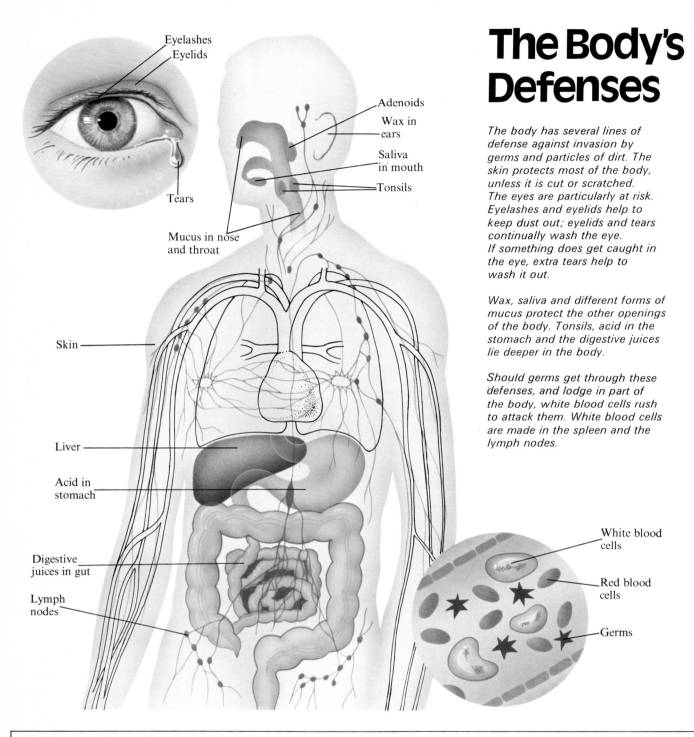

Eyelashes
Eyelids
Tears
Adenoids
Wax in ears
Saliva in mouth
Tonsils
Mucus in nose and throat
Skin
Liver
Acid in stomach
Digestive juices in gut
Lymph nodes
White blood cells
Red blood cells
Germs

The Body Fights an Invasion of Germs

Germs swim through hairs in the nose. Some are caught but others get through to start invading the rest of the body.

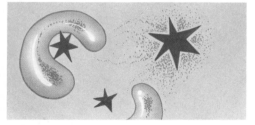

White blood cells surround germs and swallow many of them. Some germs escape and multiply.

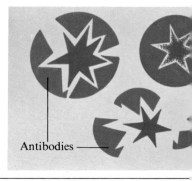

Antibodies

Our bodies are fighting disease all the time. Most of the time they win. Only when the germs that attack the body are especially powerful, do we notice the battle at all and feel ill.

The body's main external weapon is the skin. If it is unbroken very few germs can penetrate it. Cuts and open wounds make it easy for them to get in, however.

The more vulnerable parts of the body have a whole range of special defenses. The eyes are protected by eyelashes and by tears. At the back of the mouth the tonsils are on guard, and if germs get by them they usually get trapped in the mucus which lines the trachea, or destroyed by acid in the stomach.

White blood cells and antibodies

The body's second line of defense is its white blood cells. If germs do penetrate the skin, white blood cells immediately rush through the blood-stream to attack them. The white blood cells surround the germs and swallow them.

If all else fails, the body manufactures anti-bodies in the spleen and lymph nodes. Antibodies are a kind of chemical that attack the germs. The germs of each disease have to be fought by their own antibodies. Antibodies developed for another illness will not do. However, many antibodies provide the body with immunity for the rest of its life. This means that if you have had measles, for instance, you should never catch it again, because the right antibodies are ready and waiting in your body.

General health is also very important in the fight against disease. If you take regular exercise and eat the right kind of foods (see pages 18 and 38), your body will find it much easier to fight off invading germs.

Helping the body's defenses

Until quite recently, there was very little people could do to help the body to fight off disease. Then, in the late 18th century, an English country doctor called Edward Jenner discovered immunization. The principle of immunization—often also called vaccination—is simple. A healthy person absorbs a tiny quantity of the germs of a disease. The germs are either dead or still alive but very weak. They make the body produce antibodies as if it were fighting off a real disease. The dose of germs is repeated until eventually the body has produced enough antibodies to fight off the real disease should it ever attack. Immunization usually only lasts for a few years and then has to be repeated. Nowadays, in Western countries babies and small children are vaccinated against a number of diseases.

Drugs

Even more recently doctors and scientists have developed a whole range of drugs to fight disease. These are called *antibiotics*. They attack the germs in the body but not the body's cells. Penicillin, which was the first antibiotic to be discovered, in 1928, is still one of the most effective although others are also used.

▶ *An Iranian boy being vaccinated against tuberculosis. Mass vaccination campaigns have stopped many people catching some of the worst infectious diseases.*

◀ *The body begins to manufacture antibodies. Antibodies fit around the germs and stop them multiplying or harming the body. The germs then break up. Each kind of germ can only be destroyed by a particular kind of antibody. Drugs can also destroy germs, and are sometimes used to speed recovery.*

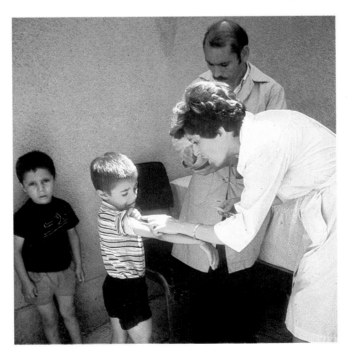

Vaccinations

Routine vaccinations include a ''triple'' vaccine (diphtheria, tetanus and whooping cough), polio, measles, rubella (German measles) and tuberculosis (BCG).
Visitors to Africa need vaccinations against yellow fever, smallpox and cholera (other vaccinations may be needed in some countries).
Visitors to South America need vaccinations against yellow fever, smallpox and cholera.
Visitors to Asia need vaccinations against smallpox and cholera (gamma globulin vaccination against hepatitis may also be given).

Infectious Diseases

◀ *Different kinds of bacteria vary in shape and size, but all are minutely small. On one square centimeter (0.15 sq.in.) of clean skin, there may be more than one million bacteria, nearly all of them harmless. There are even more bacteria—up to 1000 million per square centimeter (6500 million per sq.in.)—in the mouth, throat and intestines. Some help to digest food although some cause disease. Infectious diseases are also caused by viruses, which are even smaller than bacteria.*

▼ *Children playing together often catch colds from one another. Cold germs breathed out by one person hang in the air, and are then breathed in by someone else.*

We catch an infectious disease when our bodies are invaded by germs. There are a number of different kinds of germs. They are all so small that we can only see them under a microscope. Disease is caused by bacteria, which carry pneumonia, tetanus and cholera, or by viruses (measles, mumps, influenza), fungi or worms.

Germs reach our bodies in many different ways, through air or water, from bad food and sewage, from contact with insects, animals and other people. Many infectious diseases are far less common today than they were in the 19th century, because there are now laws which insist on high standards of health and hygiene. Housing is also better, and people no longer live so crowded together.

Nevertheless, it is still quite easy to catch the germs of an infectious disease. Every time someone with a cold sneezes, for instance, the cold viruses fall like rain over everyone nearby. (Even using a handkerchief doesn't stop them entirely!)

The course of an infectious disease

Infectious diseases pass through several stages. The first is when we are actually infected. Incubation comes next. During incubation, germs

▶ *You get food poisoning from bad food. As you start to digest the bad food, the bacteria it contains begin to attack the body giving you stomach ache.*
The body can get rid of infected food quickly by diarrhea and vomiting. Mild food poisoning clears up after a day's rest in bed. If the symptoms are very violent, or if they continue after a day or two, you should go to a doctor.

FOOD POISONING

How caught

Eating or drinking infected food

Symptoms

Sickness, diarrhea, stomach ache

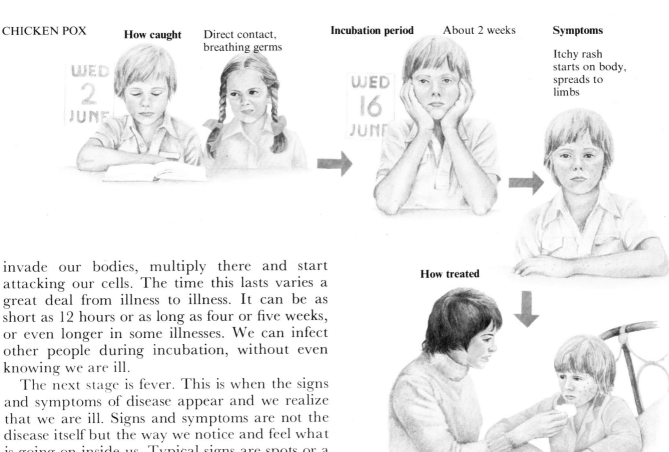

CHICKEN POX

How caught — Direct contact, breathing germs

Incubation period — About 2 weeks

Symptoms

Itchy rash starts on body, spreads to limbs

How treated

Rest. Lotion rubbed on skin to relieve irritation and stop scratching

invade our bodies, multiply there and start attacking our cells. The time this lasts varies a great deal from illness to illness. It can be as short as 12 hours or as long as four or five weeks, or even longer in some illnesses. We can infect other people during incubation, without even knowing we are ill.

The next stage is fever. This is when the signs and symptoms of disease appear and we realize that we are ill. Signs and symptoms are not the disease itself but the way we notice and feel what is going on inside us. Typical signs are spots or a rash, typical symptoms shivering and tiredness.

The fever stage is when the body starts to fight the disease in earnest. White blood cells and antibodies rush through the bloodstream to attack the germs. Because of all the extra work it is doing the body gets hotter. The heart beats faster and the pulse rate increases. People who are ill usually lose their appetite, as the body has no energy to spare for digesting food. They have to drink a lot to replace the water lost through sweating.

When the battle is won, the patient slowly begins to recover. Rest, sleep and proper food all help in regaining strength.

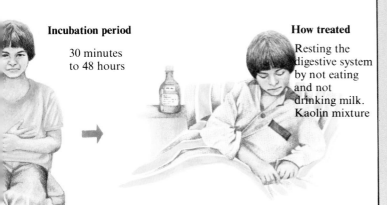

Incubation period

30 minutes to 48 hours

How treated

Resting the digestive system by not eating and not drinking milk. Kaolin mixture

---

Different kinds of food poisoning

Poisoning by bacteria

Salmonellae are very common. Often infect farm animals which can lead to contamination of food. Easily killed by heat.

Shigellae cause dysentery. Live in man and spread by direct or indirect contact. Killed by heat or disinfectants.

Staphylococci are common parasites living in man. Killed by ordinary cooking temperatures.

Clostridium welchii lives in soil and also on flies which spread it to food. Destroyed by cooking.

Clostridium botulinum lives in soil or decaying vegetation. Caused by faulty canning. Killed by heat. Can cause death.

Vibrio parahemolyticus found in seawater. Can get into fish and shellfish. Killed by cooking.

Bacillus cereus is found in dust, soil and on green vegetables and potatoes. Killed by cooking at high temperatures.

Metallic or chemical poisoning can occur when metal from a pan or container seeps into the food it contains.

Mushroom poisoning is caused by dangerous fungi (not mushrooms). Can cause death.

Mussel poisoning is caused by dinoflagellates, minute organisms which sometimes live in mussels.

Hospitals

Many people think of hospitals as places where doctors and nurses wage a desperate and dramatic battle to save a patient's life. That picture is true, but it is only a small part of what really happens in a hospital.

People who are ill go to the hospital because they need care that they cannot receive at home. If all they need is rest and warmth while a fever works itself out, then they can stay at home quite safely if there is someone to look after them. If their illness is more serious, however, they have to go into hospital to be looked after by experts.

Surgery

Some illnesses require surgery. This involves surgeons—doctors who have specialized in one type of medicine—cutting a patient's body open so that they can do repair work inside. Some surgery is very simple, such as removing tonsils or the appendix, and the patient must stay in the hospital for only a few days after the operation. Other operations are much more complicated. They last longer and the patient must remain longer in the hospital before being allowed to go home.

Among the most difficult operations nowadays is "spare-part" surgery. This is when surgeons try to replace a part of a patient's body that is no longer working. They either use an artificial substitute, or a healthy organ taken from someone who has just died.

Surgery must take place in a hospital. To prevent the patient becoming infected, all the equipment used in the operation must be sterilized first. Doctors and nurses have to wash very well before an operation. This is called *scrubbing up.*

Casualty

Most large hospitals also have casualty wards. These are for people who are taken ill suddenly or who have been involved in an accident. Doctors and nurses on duty in the casualty ward are ready to look after patients as soon as they are brought in.

Preventing illness

Preventing people becoming ill is just as important as curing them when they are ill. Many people who visit a hospital are not ill at all. Doctors give them a check-up to make sure that nothing is wrong and also advise them on how to stay healthy. People who have been ill also have to go to hospital for a check-up from time to time.

▼This person is having her chest X-rayed to check whether she is suffering from TB (tuberculosis). Such checks can detect a disease before it becomes serious.

▼People with arthritic hands like these shown here may come to hospital regularly for physiotherapy. This treatment helps to bring some strength back to their hands. A badly affected hip joint may be replaced by a metal ball and socket.

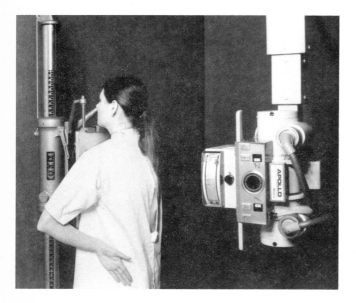
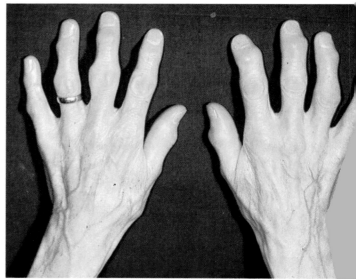

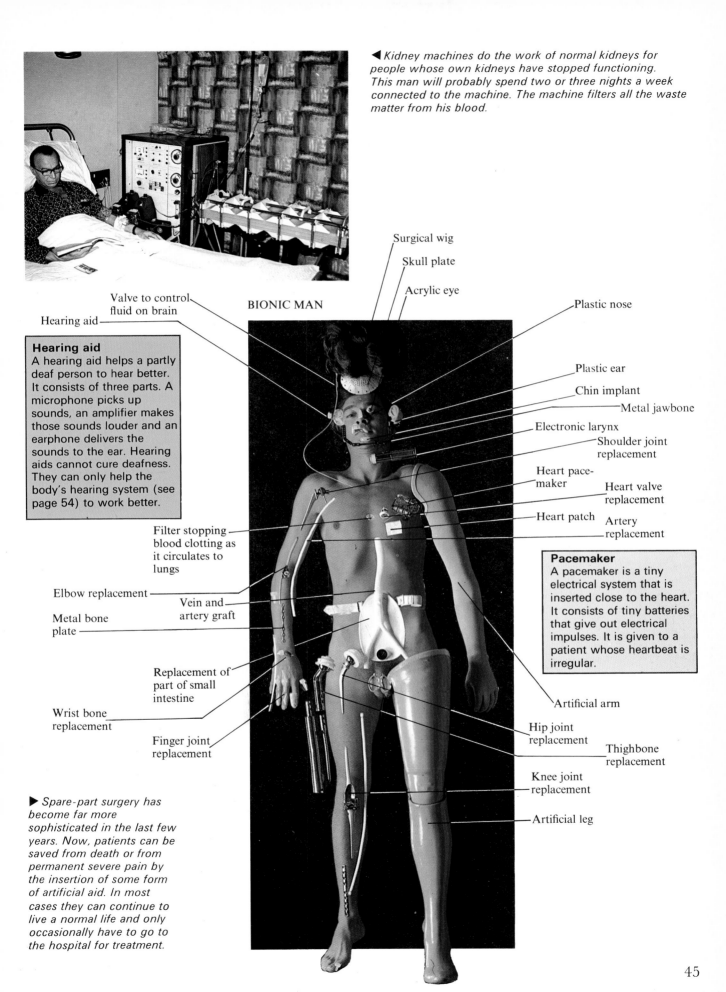

◀ Kidney machines do the work of normal kidneys for people whose own kidneys have stopped functioning. This man will probably spend two or three nights a week connected to the machine. The machine filters all the waste matter from his blood.

Surgical wig

Skull plate

Acrylic eye

BIONIC MAN

Plastic nose

Valve to control fluid on brain

Hearing aid

Plastic ear

Chin implant

Metal jawbone

Electronic larynx

Shoulder joint replacement

Hearing aid
A hearing aid helps a partly deaf person to hear better. It consists of three parts. A microphone picks up sounds, an amplifier makes those sounds louder and an earphone delivers the sounds to the ear. Hearing aids cannot cure deafness. They can only help the body's hearing system (see page 54) to work better.

Heart pace-maker

Heart valve replacement

Heart patch

Artery replacement

Filter stopping blood clotting as it circulates to lungs

Elbow replacement

Vein and artery graft

Pacemaker
A pacemaker is a tiny electrical system that is inserted close to the heart. It consists of tiny batteries that give out electrical impulses. It is given to a patient whose heartbeat is irregular.

Metal bone plate

Replacement of part of small intestine

Wrist bone replacement

Finger joint replacement

Artificial arm

Hip joint replacement

Thighbone replacement

Knee joint replacement

Artificial leg

▶ Spare-part surgery has become far more sophisticated in the last few years. Now, patients can be saved from death or from permanent severe pain by the insertion of some form of artificial aid. In most cases they can continue to live a normal life and only occasionally have to go to the hospital for treatment.

Chapter Five

Coordination

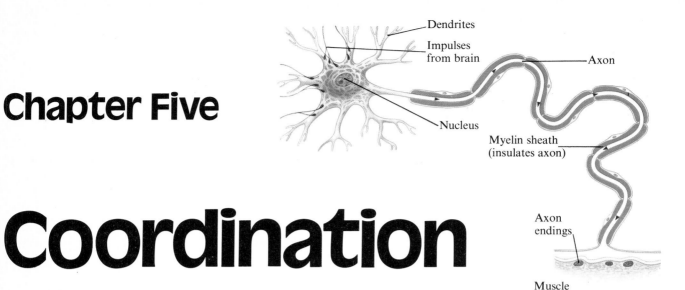

Dendrites
Impulses from brain
Axon
Nucleus
Myelin sheath (insulates axon)
Axon endings
Muscle

▲ *A much enlarged view of a motor nerve, with its many dendrites and long axon. Motor nerves conduct messages in the form of electrical impulses, which travel very fast from the brain to the muscles to make them contract.*

The previous chapters in this book have described how the inside of the body operates, how it fights off attacks from outside in the form of disease and how a new life is made. But there would be little point in these things happening on their own. They are only useful in so far as they enable our bodies to survive in the world outside.

To function in the outside world—that is, to think and behave and act and have emotions and opinions—we depend on the brain and the nervous system. The nervous system provides us with thousands of points of contact with the outside world. It enables us to see and hear, to taste and smell, to feel pain and to sense heat and cold and pressure. On its own, however, the nervous system is incomplete. All it does is receive sensations from the outside world and dispatch them along the nerves to the brain.

It is the brain that translates the information provided by the nervous system into something that we can use. When you look at the words on this page, your eyes receive an image—two images, in fact, because you have two eyes—which is transmitted to the brain. But it is the brain that merges those images and tells you what they represent. And it does more than that. It also enables you to understand and think about what the words mean.

In fact the brain is an enormous store containing everything we have ever experienced. Far, far more quickly even than a computer, it can coordinate the information provided by the nervous system, sort through the millions of experiences it has stored up and tell us how to react to a particular situation. And if it needs to instruct the body to do something, it does so through the nervous system once again.

The brain also controls the workings of the inside of the body through the autonomic nervous system (see page 48). In this part of its work, it is helped by the glands. When necessary, these produce chemicals called hormones (see page 58) that travel through the bloodstream to different parts of the body.

▶ *Tracy Austin, the young tennis player, poised to return her opponent's shot. To do this, she will use many muscles. These will be put into action by messages passed by the nervous system from the brain to the muscles.*

A SPINAL REFLEX

THE NERVOUS SYSTEM

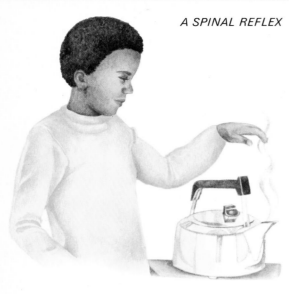

▲When the steam from the hot kettle reaches this girl's hand, a message is immediately flashed along the sensory nerves to her spinal cord.

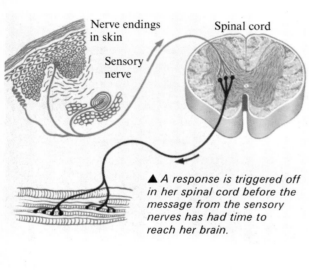

Nerve endings in skin

Sensory nerve

Spinal cord

▲ A response is triggered off in her spinal cord before the message from the sensory nerves has had time to reach her brain.

▲ A message to remove her hand immediately returns along the motor nerve.

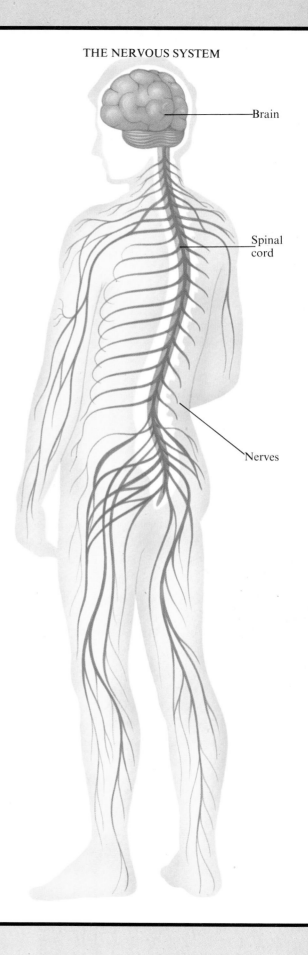

Brain

Spinal cord

Nerves

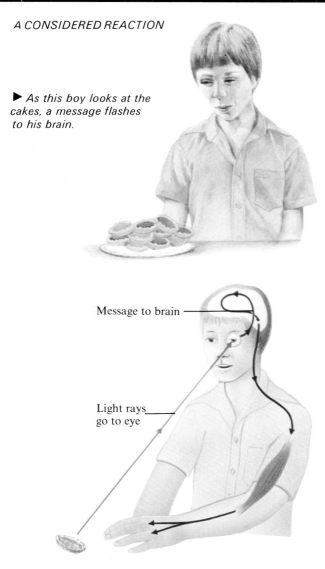

▶ As this boy looks at the cakes, a message flashes to his brain.

Message to brain

Light rays go to eye

▲ He wonders whether to eat a cake. He decides he will and his brain sends out appropriate messages along his motor nerves.

The messages sent along his motor nerves tell him to move his fingers, pick up the cake and start eating it.

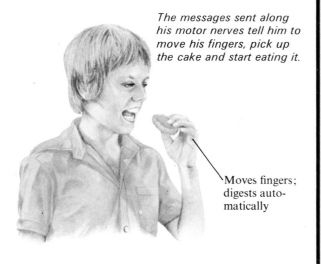

Moves fingers; digests auto-matically

Nerves and Reflexes

The nervous system links the body with the brain. Whenever the body reacts to something—pain, maybe, or heat—the nervous system informs the brain. In turn, the brain uses the nervous system to tell the body what to do.

There are nerves in every part of our body. Those in the head and neck lead directly to the brain. Those in the rest of the body meet in the spinal cord which leads to the brain.

How nerves work

If someone throws a stone at you, you move out of its way. Your eyes see the stone being thrown and immediately transmit a message to the brain along the nerve leading from the eye to the brain. The brain absorbs the information and sends messages through the nervous system to the muscles of the feet and legs, telling them to move.

Nerves are made of bundles of fiber. These become smaller and smaller the nearer they get to the nerve endings. Small nerve fibers are either sensory or motor. Sensory nerves transmit messages to the brain. Motor nerves transmit messages from the brain to the muscles. Larger nerves contain both sensory and motor fibers. The actual cells that carry the messages are called neurones.

Reflexes

Some of our actions really are automatic. These are called *reflexes*. If something burns your fingers you move them away immediately. Your nerves feel the pain and immediately flash messages along the sensory nerves. These get a response as soon as they reach the spinal cord, when the motor nerves tell the fingers to move away from the heat. The sensory nerves continue to transmit the messages to the brain, but the necessary action has already been taken.

The autonomic nervous system

The autonomic nervous system controls many of our internal systems, such as digestion, the circulatory system, breathing and so on. It operates independently of the other nerves in the body, and, however hard we try, we normally have no conscious control over it.

The Brain

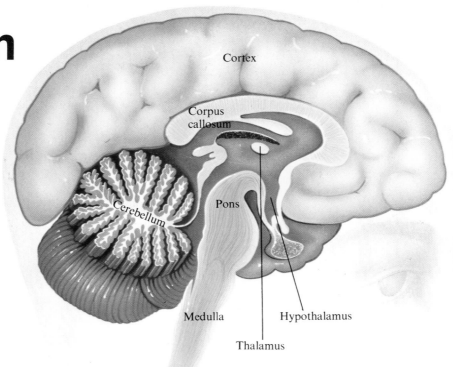

Cortex

Corpus callosum

Cerebellum

Pons

Medulla

Hypothalamus

Thalamus

INSIDE THE BRAIN

The Cortex forms 80% of the brain. It is made up of "gray matter" – 10,000 million nerve cells. It is responsible for intelligence, memory, thought and all conscious processes

The Corpus callosum is a mass of nerve fibers (white matter) connecting the two halves of the cortex

The Pons (bridge) links the cortex with the cerebellum

The Cerebellum (little brain) controls balance and coordination

The Medulla contains groups of nerve cells that control breathing and heart rates, and digestion. Because nerves from the spinal cord cross over on their way through the medulla, the left part of the brain controls the right part of the body and *vice versa*

The Thalamus receives and processes signals from the body's sensory system before passing them to the cortex

The Hypothalamus controls the body's temperature and the amount of salt and water in the blood. It also forms a link between the hormone and nervous systems and is concerned with emotions and body rhythms

The brain is the body's control center. It receives information from every part of the body through the sensory nerves. It then organizes that information, decides what to do and sends out orders to every part of the body through the motor nerves.

Some of the brain's decisions are relatively simple, like the example on page 49, when the sensory nerves warned that a stone was being thrown and the brain passed a message to the legs and feet to move out of the way. But most of its work is far more complicated than that. The brain also organizes the memory, thinking and the emotions. Sometimes, walking down a street, you catch sight of someone you think you know. Your eyes transmit what you see to the brain and you try to "place" this person—remind yourself where it was you met her—was it at school, at a party, at a youth group? Then you suddenly remember where you met her, what you did, and what you talked about, and you also feel pleased (or sorry!) to see her.

Inside the brain

The brain weighs about 1.3 kg (2.9 lb) and contains about 14 thousand million cells, each completely separate. The cells receive information from the sensory nerves in the form of electrical impulses, and they send out orders to the motor nerves in the same form. No one knows exactly how the information is moved from cell to cell within the brain—that is, exactly how the memory works. Scientists think that it has something to do with changes in the chemical make-up of the cells.

The brain is divided up into several different parts, each with its own job to do. The most significant of these, and also the largest, is the cortex. This is where intelligence, memory and thought all originate.

The cortex is divided into two halves, or hemispheres. Each of these has four lobes. The frontal lobe controls the motor nerves. Different parts of the motor area are linked to different sets of muscles. Much of the rest of the frontal lobe

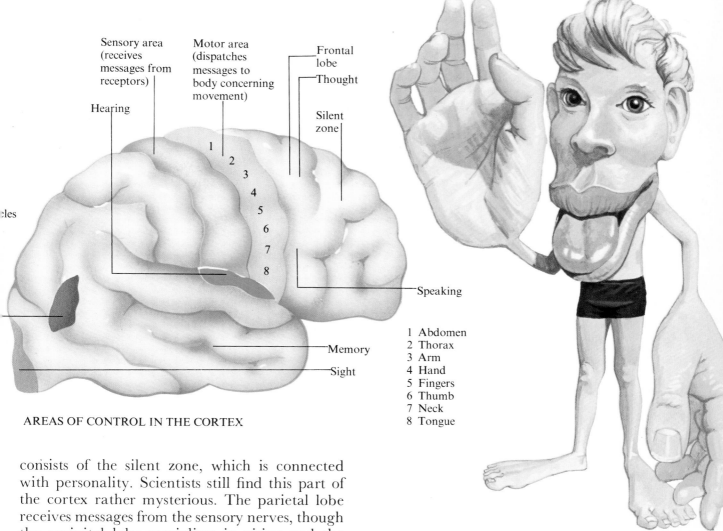

▼ *Different parts of the body are linked to different parts of the cortex, as shown in the illustration below. In the illustration on the right the body has been redrawn to show the area of the cortex devoted to each part.*

Sensory area (receives messages from receptors)

Motor area (dispatches messages to body concerning movement)

Frontal lobe

Thought

Silent zone

Hearing

1
2
3
4
5
6
7
8

Speaking

Memory

Sight

1 Abdomen
2 Thorax
3 Arm
4 Hand
5 Fingers
6 Thumb
7 Neck
8 Tongue

AREAS OF CONTROL IN THE CORTEX

consists of the silent zone, which is connected with personality. Scientists still find this part of the cortex rather mysterious. The parietal lobe receives messages from the sensory nerves, though the occipital lobe specializes in vision and the temporal lobe in hearing.

The left hemisphere of the cortex controls the right-hand side of the body, and the right hemisphere the body's left side. Usually the left hemisphere is dominant, which explains why most people are right-handed—and right-footed.

The hypothalamus

Another important, but much smaller, part of the brain is the hypothalamus. Though it only takes up about one three-hundredth of the brain, it is the control center for the autonomic nervous system (see page 49). This means that it regulates all the body's automatic internal functions, its temperature, appetite and thirst, the amount of salt and water in the blood and the pituitary gland (see page 58).

Brain damage

The brain needs a continual supply of blood to feed it food and oxygen. An interruption of only a few seconds will damage some of its cells, and after a few minutes it will stop working entirely.

If part of someone's brain is damaged, the part of the body which it controls becomes paralyzed and cannot work. Proper messages cannot be passed along the nerves to the muscles concerned, or speech or hearing are affected. If someone is disabled in an accident and one or more of their nerves is damaged, those nerves will not be able to pass messages to and from the brain. As a result the parts of the body to which they lead cannot be used.

INSIDE THE EYE

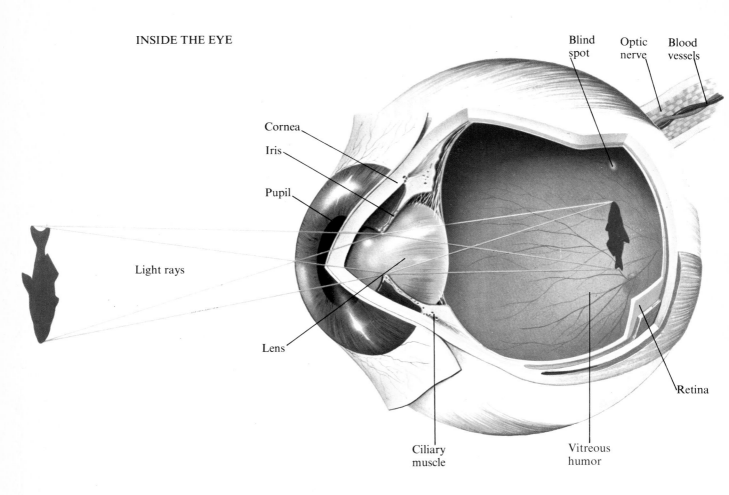

Blind spot

Optic nerve

Blood vessels

Cornea

Iris

Pupil

Light rays

Lens

Ciliary muscle

Vitreous humor

Retina

BLIND SPOT

One part of the eye, the optic nerve head, does not contain any nerve endings and so cannot actually see anything. You can find this blind spot by holding this book in front of you, closing your right eye and staring at the spot with your left eye. Slowly move the book toward your eye, and eventually the cat will disappear.

THINGS TO DO

What happens to your eyes in the dark?
Look in a mirror and close your eyes until they are nearly shut. Your pupils get bigger so that they let in more light. This is what happens when you go out at night. Open your eyes quickly, and you'll see your pupils shrinking. This means that less light is being let in, because in bright light the eyes need less light.

Are you right-eyed or left-eyed?
Point your finger at an object in the distance. Then close your left eye and see whether your finger is still pointing at the object. Now do the same thing with your right eye. If your finger moved while your left eye was closed, then your right eye is stronger, and *vice versa*.

LONG SIGHT

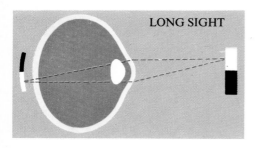

Long sight means that the eye can focus on distant objects, but that nearby ones produce an image behind the retina. Spectacles or contact lenses with a convex lens make the rays focus further forward.

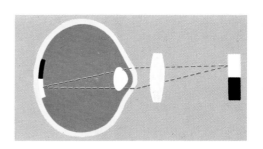

52

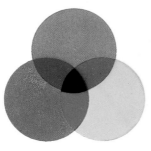

Red, blue and yellow are the primary paint colors. A combination of all three mixed together produces the color black.

Red, green and blue are the primary light colors. Any colored light can be produced by mixing together different amounts of these. When all three are mixed together, white light is produced.

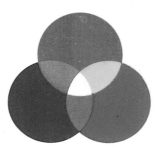

▼ *Look at this strangely-colored American flag for 30 seconds without blinking. Then look at a piece of white paper. You should see the flag in its correct colors. After you have stared at the flag for a while, your eyes get tired of seeing blue, yellow and black and instead you see their complementary colors, red, blue and white.*

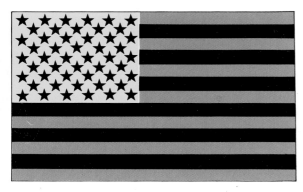

Sight

Seeing things is a complicated process that involves both the eyes and the brain. Thousands of rays of light from the objects around us enter our eyes all the time.

The rays pass through the cornea, the pupil and the lens and finally reach the retina. First the cornea and the liquid in the eye, and then the lens focus them, so that the retina sees a single image of what the eye is looking at, not a confused mixture of images. The iris, which surrounds the pupil, controls the amount of light that is let in through the pupil. In bright light, the iris contracts, so that less light can pass through the pupil. In dim light the iris enlarges the pupil.

The retina, which consists of millions of nerve endings, doesn't actually do our seeing for us. Instead the nerve endings put the images they receive into a code that can be passed along the optic nerve to the brain. These coded images are very small and upside down. They are also in three colors only and in two dimensions.

Because we have two eyes, the brain receives two sets of images. Each of these is slightly different, since our eyes look at things from different angles. The brain puts all the information it receives together and turns it into what we actually see.

The nerve endings in the retina are called light receptors. There are two types, rods and cones. Rods see things only in black and white and are used in dull light. Cones distinguish three colors, red, green and blue. They only work in bright light, during the day or in artificial light. Though the messages they send to the brain are in just three colors, the combination of messages can be translated into 150 to 200 different shades.

People who are color blind cannot distinguish between some colors. Color blindness usually results from faulty cones.

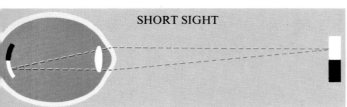

SHORT SIGHT

▲ *Short sight means that the light rays focus in front of the retina. You can focus nearby objects but not distant*

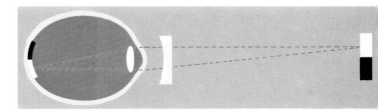

ones. Spectacles or contact lenses with a concave lens diverge the rays slightly, and make the rays focus further back.

Hearing and Balance

The ear has three parts. The part we can actually see—the outer ear, or pinna—is the least important. Though it helps to catch and direct the noises, or sound waves, we hear, we could still hear without it.

Hearing works in stages. One stage starts as the previous one finishes, though we are not aware of any delay. Sound waves travel down the auditory canal to the eardrum. This forms a barrier between the outer and the middle ear. When the waves reach the eardrum, it begins to vibrate. This then makes three small bones (the hammer, anvil and stirrup) inside the middle ear vibrate. They in their turn set off vibrations in the oval window, which is the barrier between the middle ear and the inner ear.

The inner ear consists of a tube called the cochlea which is filled with fluid. The cochlea contains the cells at the end of the auditory nerve. The vibrations of the oval window cause the fluid in the cochlea to vibrate, which stimulates the nerve cells to send messages to the brain.

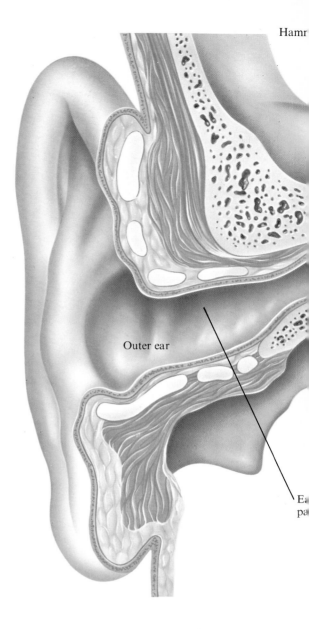

Outer ear

E
pa

Deafness
Deafness can result from an infection in the ear, although some people are also born deaf. Sometimes the reason for this is genetic, although it can be caused if the mother has German measles during pregnancy or if the baby suffers from a lack of oxygen during its birth. Deaf aids nearly always improve a deaf person's hearing, as they can be suited to the type of deafness from which a person suffers. Aids are not selective, however. The human ear cuts out many of the sounds in which it is not interested, whereas a deaf aid makes them all louder.

◄ Hearing can be damaged very easily so people who work in noisy surroundings, like these racing car mechanics, wear ear muffs to protect their hearing.

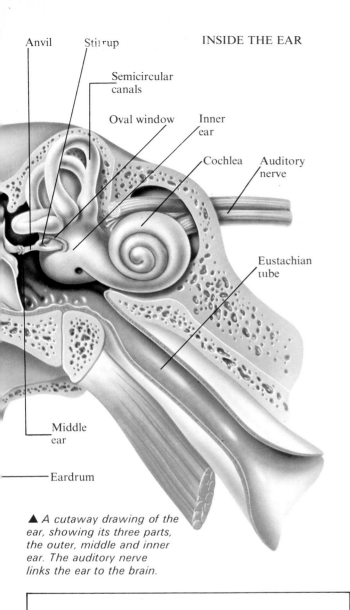

Anvil   Stirrup

Semicircular canals

Oval window   Inner ear

Cochlea   Auditory nerve

Eustachian tube

Middle ear

Eardrum

▲ *A cutaway drawing of the ear, showing its three parts, the outer, middle and inner ear. The auditory nerve links the ear to the brain.*

How noisy is it?

The ear is a very sensitive instrument. It can hear very soft and very loud sounds and high and low ones too. Many animals, however, can hear a far greater range of sound.

Because they are so sensitive, ears can be damaged very easily. Noise is measured in units called decibels. Noises of more than 165 decibels can be fatal but frequent exposure to much quieter noises can also damage hearing.

	Noise over 80 decibels is dangerous
Normal breathing	
Whisper	
Conversation	
Busy traffic	
Vacuum cleaner	
Subway train	
Decibels (approx)	Pop group at $1\frac{1}{2}$ meters (4ft)
	Jet fighter taking off

0 10 20 30 40 50 60 70 80 90 100 110 120 130

Some of the nerve cells in the cochlea pick up high sounds, others low sounds.

It is the brain that sorts out the messages it receives from both our ears and tells us what we are hearing.

Balance

The ears have a second very important function. They provide the brain with the information that enables us to keep our balance.

Inside each inner ear there are three semicircular canals filled with fluid. Two are vertical, one horizontal. The insides of the canals are lined with nerve endings. As you move your head, the fluid moves in turn and presses against the nerve endings, which transmit messages to the brain. In addition, two sacs, called the *saccule* and the *utricle*, inform the brain what angle your head is at to the vertical. Without them, you would not be able to keep your balance when moving around.

Balance is also helped by the eyes and by nerve endings in the muscles, joints and feet.

▼ *Olympic gymnast champion Nadia Comaneci balancing on the beam. It can take years of practice to balance as well as she does.*

Taste and Smell

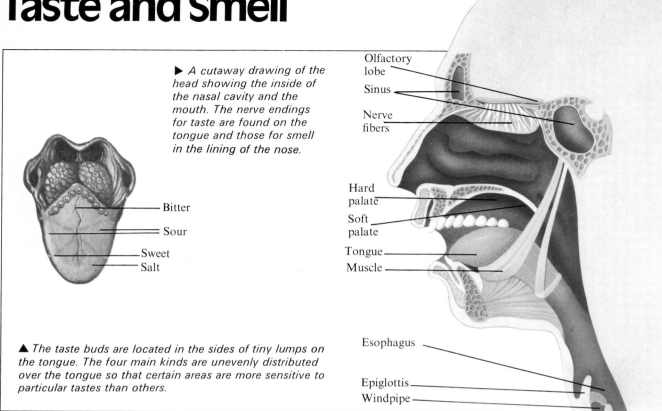

▶ *A cutaway drawing of the head showing the inside of the nasal cavity and the mouth. The nerve endings for taste are found on the tongue and those for smell in the lining of the nose.*

Bitter
Sour
Sweet
Salt

Olfactory lobe
Sinus
Nerve fibers
Hard palate
Soft palate
Tongue
Muscle
Esophagus
Epiglottis
Windpipe

▲ *The taste buds are located in the sides of tiny lumps on the tongue. The four main kinds are unevenly distributed over the tongue so that certain areas are more sensitive to particular tastes than others.*

Taste is picked up by taste buds. There are about 10,000 of these. Most of them are on the tongue, but there are also a few on the pharynx, palate and nostrils. Taste buds consist of tiny clusters of cells. These are the ends of nerves that lead to the brain.

There are only four main tastes, sweet, sour, bitter and salty. Different tastes affect different taste buds. The buds for sweet and salt tastes are at the front of the tongue, those for sour at the sides and those for bitter at the back. Solid foods cannot be tasted until they have been partially dissolved by saliva.

Smell

Our sense of smell is far more sophisticated than our sense of taste. We may say that a meal "tastes" good. In fact, we can only taste the four

sensations mentioned above. What makes it "taste" so delicious is our sense of smell. If you have a cold and your nose gets blocked, it becomes very difficult to taste food.

The sense of smell lies in the olfactory cells. These are at the back and top of the nose and consist of tiny cilia covered with mucus. The cilia are the ends of nerves leading to the brain. When we breathe normally, some air passes the olfactory cells, but to smell properly we have to wrinkle up our noses and sniff. This forces the air up to the mucus and so stimulates the nerve endings.

Most human beings can detect several thousand smells, although some people can identify more. People are very poor smellers in comparison with animals, however. Dogs' noses, for instance, are over a million times more sensitive.

Testing the sense of smell
Take one teaspoonful each of ginger, cinnamon, mustard, pepper, peppermint extract and lemon juice. Then get your friends to come in one by one blindfolded, and see if they can tell which is which just by smelling them. Then mix two of the smells together—perhaps the mustard and pepper—and see if your friends can still distinguish them.

Testing the sense of taste
Take one teaspoonful each of flour, confectioner's sugar, cocoa powder and a flavored milkshake powder. Get your friends to come in blindfolded, give them a bit of each to taste and see if they can guess what each is. Then make them hold their noses and see if they can still guess correctly.

Touch and Pain

The body can respond to five different kinds of touch. These are light touch, or contact, heavy touch, or pressure, heat, cold and pain. Nerve cells, or receptors, all over the body pick up these sensations and transmit them along nerves to the brain. Some cells can only sense one kind of touch, while others can sense more than one. Pain can also be felt in free nerve endings all over the body.

There are more pain receptors than any other kind. Next numerous are light and heavy touch, then heat and cold. This means that we can say where we feel pain much more precisely than where we feel cold. Some parts of the body, like the tongue, lips and fingertips, are much more sensitive to touch than others.

There are also numerous touch receptors inside the body. These help to keep it functioning. Most of the time we do not even realize they are working, though we do feel some of the sensations, such as hunger and tiredness, they produce.

Pain

When the skin is lightly brushed, the epidermis begins to itch. When pain receptors in the dermis are stimulated, a sharp pain results. An aching pain originates much deeper in the dermis.

Pain warns us that something has gone wrong or that something is about to go wrong. Being able to feel pain is an important biological advantage. Pain makes people move quickly or automatically away from danger (such as in touching something hot). But just because we are not feeling any pain it does not necessarily mean that our bodies are functioning properly. Some things go wrong without causing pain. In addition, the amount of pain we feel has nothing to do with how seriously we are hurt.

Pain is not the same thing as a hurt. If our fingers get burnt, for instance, they are hurt and damaged, but the sensation of pain is felt in the mind. This is why some people seem to feel pain more, or less, than others. Pain is a sensation produced by the brain once it has been stimulated by the pain receptors.

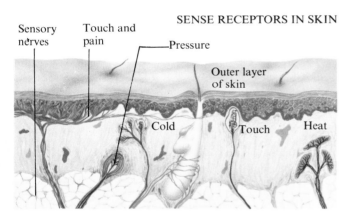

SENSE RECEPTORS IN SKIN

Sensory nerves — Touch and pain — Pressure — Outer layer of skin — Cold — Touch — Heat

▲ Different types of receptors in the skin deal with particular sensations.

Two-point touch
You can discover how sensitive different parts of the body are by touching them with a pair of dividers. Set the points 5 mm ($\frac{1}{4}$ in.) apart and try touching various parts of your body with them. Only your fingertips, nose and tongue will register that there are two points. The rest of the body will feel them as one. The middle of the tongue is the most sensitive part of the body, the middle of the back the least.

► Firewalkers walking through flames at a festival in Hong Kong. The flames do not harm them at all and they feel no pain. Because pain is felt in the brain and not the body, people respond differently to it. Some women, for example, find childbirth more painful than others.

Hormones

▶ Shortly before her baby is born, hormones stimulate the production of milk in a mother's breasts.

Hormones are chemical substances that help to control the internal workings of the body. They are stored in glands and are released automatically into the bloodstream when they are needed. The bloodstream carries them throughout the body. Nerves carry messages quickly between the brain and particular parts of the body. Hormones usually act more slowly and over a much longer period of time. They may carry messages that affect many parts of the body.

The main glands are the pituitary, thyroid and parathyroid, the adrenals, the pancreas and the reproductive glands. The adrenals work in a slightly different way from the others and are discussed on pages 60–61.

The pituitary gland

The pituitary gland produces its own hormones and also controls all the other glands.

The pituitary gland produces the growth hormone. This travels through the bloodstream to every part of the body and makes us grow. It is produced throughout childhood and in especially large quantities during puberty (see page 32), when it stimulates the growth of the reproductive glands.

The pituitary gland also produces the anti-diuretic hormone. This controls the amount of water our kidneys return to the body, and how much they allow to leave the body as urine.

As well as producing its own hormones, the pituitary gland manufactures what are called *trophic* hormones. These stimulate the other glands into producing their own hormones. The system works automatically. The pituitary gland stimulates the thyroid gland, for example, into activity. When the thyroid gland has produced enough hormones of its own, they automatically suppress the trophic hormones, until the cycle starts all over again.

The pituitary gland, which is situated under the brain, is controlled by the brain and the nervous system. A nerve center in the brain reports if there are not enough hormones in the blood and the brain informs the pituitary gland.

The other glands

The hormones produced by the thyroid gland determine how quickly food is broken down into energy and heat for the body's cells. They have nothing to do with the actual breakdown, however. The thyroid hormones are called thyroxine and are vital to the growth of the body and the nervous system.

The parathyroid glands control the amount of calcium in the body.

The hormones produced by the pancreas are called insulin. Insulin controls the amount of sugar in the blood. People who have too much or too little insulin suffer from diabetes. This is a very serious disease, but it can usually be controlled quite easily.

The reproductive glands produce sex hormones which bring about the changes to the body at the start of puberty.

All the other glands in the body are controlled by the pituitary gland.

▶ This illustration shows the location of the endocrine glands in the body. Both testes and ovaries have been indicated, although they would not be present in the same body.

▲ A diabetic girl injecting herself with insulin. Diabetes is an illness caused by a lack of insulin (a hormone produced by the pancreas) in the blood. Diabetics must not eat too much carbohydrate and must eat regularly.

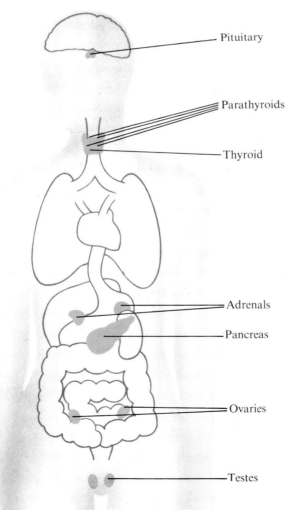

Pituitary

Parathyroids

Thyroid

Adrenals

Pancreas

Ovaries

Testes

▲ The hormone which stimulates body growth, is produced by the pituitary gland. Very tall people, like the well-known basketball star Wilt Chamberlain, who is 2.1 meters (7 feet 1 inch) tall, have received a large amount of the growth hormone. Mohammed Ali looks small beside him.

The growth of body and facial hair in men is stimulated during puberty by the production of a hormone called testosterone.

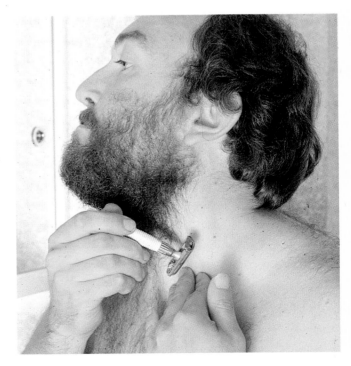

The Emergency Hormone

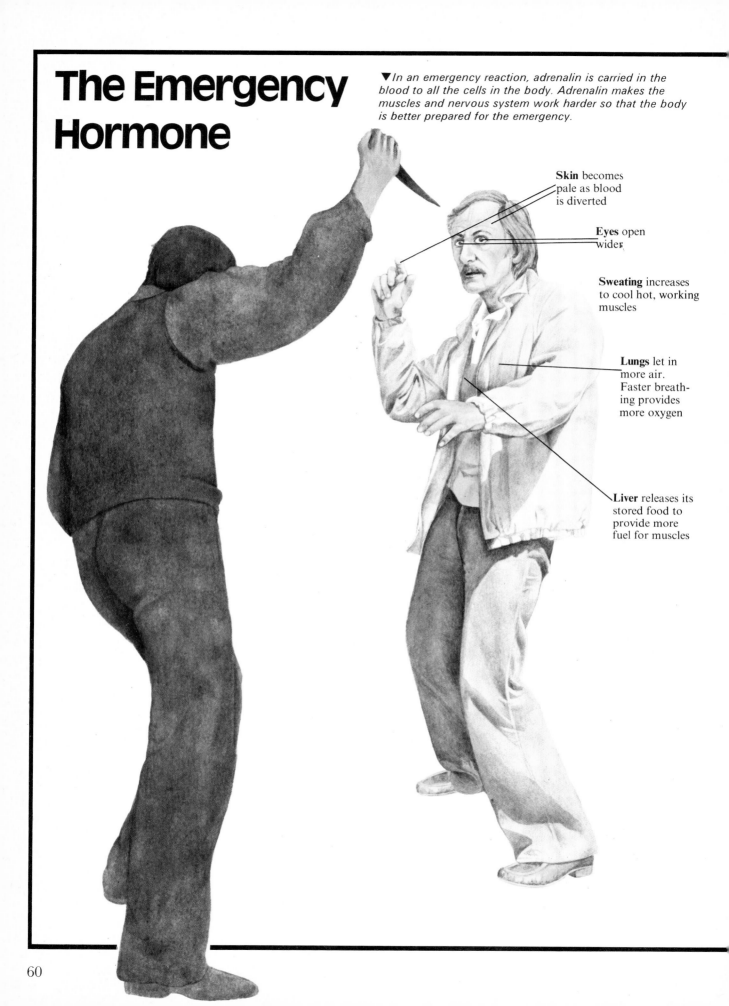

▼In an emergency reaction, adrenalin is carried in the blood to all the cells in the body. Adrenalin makes the muscles and nervous system work harder so that the body is better prepared for the emergency.

Skin becomes pale as blood is diverted

Eyes open wider

Sweating increases to cool hot, working muscles

Lungs let in more air. Faster breathing provides more oxygen

Liver releases its stored food to provide more fuel for muscles

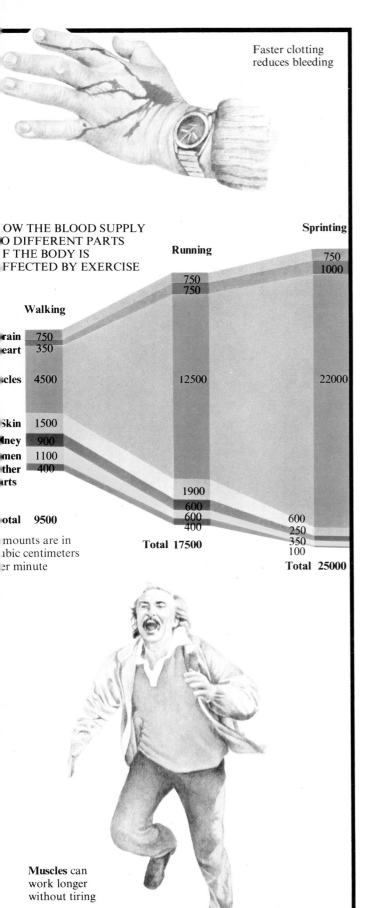

Faster clotting reduces bleeding

HOW THE BLOOD SUPPLY TO DIFFERENT PARTS OF THE BODY IS AFFECTED BY EXERCISE

	Walking	Running	Sprinting
Brain	750	750	750
Heart	350	750	1000
Muscles	4500	12500	22000
Skin	1500	1900	600
Kidney	900	600	250
Abdomen	1100	600	350
Other parts	400	400	100
Total	9500	Total 17500	Total 25000

Amounts are in cubic centimeters per minute

Muscles can work longer without tiring

The adrenal glands produce two hormones, noradrenalin and adrenalin. Noradrenalin is used for routine jobs in the body, such as keeping the blood pressure constant, while adrenalin acts in emergencies. When the body is calm, slightly more noradrenalin than adrenalin is produced, but in an emergency, far more adrenalin than noradrenalin is produced.

The brain reacts to unusual situations and to emotions such as fear and anger by stimulating the pituitary gland. As explained on pages 58-59, the pituitary gland sends trophic hormones through the blood to the adrenal glands. These respond by pouring out much larger quantities of adrenalin than usual.

The effect is immediate. The heart beats faster so that blood moves round the body more quickly. Some blood is temporarily diverted from the digestive system and the skin (which can do with less for short periods) to the muscles so that they receive more food and oxygen. This is why people go pale in tense situations, as blood drains from their skin. The extra food and oxygen enable the muscles to work more efficiently.

The rate of breathing also increases, so that the lungs take in more oxygen. Nostrils flare, to allow more air to enter, and the chest heaves. At the same time more glucose is released into the bloodstream, so that the body is provided with more energy.

All this prepares the body for sudden action. All its energies can be concentrated on coping with the emergency.

The way in which the body meets the emergency makes no difference to its reactions. They are the same whether the response is fight or flight, that is, whether we stand and face up to the emergency or take avoiding action.

The expression fight or flight can be a little misleading. Fear and anger are not the only emotions the adrenal glands respond to. They also act in situations such as a rolling ship, when the brain receives messages from the eyes which do not match the messages it receives from the rest of the body. All feelings of tension or excitement—perhaps before an examination, or before taking part in a public event, such as a school concert—are the result of an increased supply of adrenalin. Nor are these feelings always entirely involuntary. Athletes, for instance, will deliberately wind themselves up before a big race, in order that their bodies will work as efficiently as possible.

Chapter Six

Under-standing the World

◀ Discovering how the world and everything in it works is an important and fascinating part of growing up.

▶ Maps are one way of making sense of the world. These maps represent the streets and underground railway system of London. You have to be able to understand and read maps before they can be of any use to you.

The brain and the nervous system are the equipment we use to understand the world, just as the brakes, clutch, steering wheel, accelerator and so on are the equipment necessary to drive a car. But on their own they are useless. We first have to learn how to make use of the information the brain and the nervous system tell us, just as driving a car means knowing how and when to use the different controls.

The memory is the key to understanding the world. We store most of the information provided by the brain and the nervous system in the memory. It is like an enormous filing cabinet in which our past experiences are kept until we need them. When we think and make decisions, we use the information and ideas stored there.

It may seem that we remember most things automatically. But in fact much of what we remember has to be learned. By exploration,

trial and error, practice and reasoning, we gradually come to understand much about the world we live in. We can use past experiences to help us cope with new ones. Some things we learn almost without realizing it, such as our names. Other things take a lot of practice and effort, such as learning to speak a foreign language.

Much of the world around us remains a mystery. We do not know why we dream, for instance, and how the mind creates seemingly impossible events as we sleep. Nor do we understand why some people seem to be able to communicate without using the usual senses, by telepathy, for example.

A Baby's World

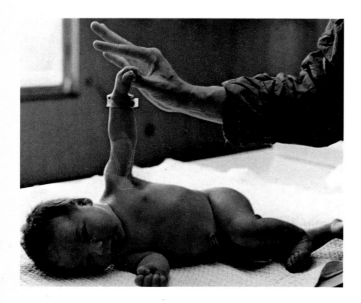

▲ Babies are born with a few basic skills. One of them is the ability to grip. For the first two months of its life, a baby's grip is strong enough to lift its whole body.

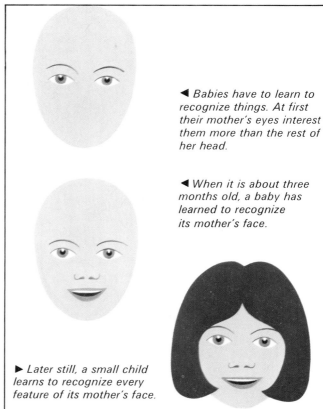

◄ Babies have to learn to recognize things. At first their mother's eyes interest them more than the rest of her head.

◄ When it is about three months old, a baby has learned to recognize its mother's face.

► Later still, a small child learns to recognize every feature of its mother's face.

A newborn baby has to rely on its parents for all the things it needs. It not only needs food and warmth and other physical things, but must also have its mother's love and support. Babies have very strong feelings for their mother and if she leaves them for too long they may become angry and frightened. Babies are weak and easily hurt.

The world outside

A baby knows nothing about the world at first. It has to learn about things. Once it is old enough to crawl, it can explore all the objects it can reach. But even before this the baby will explore its mother's face and will touch things and even suck them to get to know them better. At first, it may dislike strangers, but after a while the baby will stare at an unfamiliar person, trying to fit them into the world it knows.

As the months go by, the baby learns more and more skills. This means using past experiences to work out problems and take decisions. During this time it is growing fast, and its muscles are developing. Soon it can toddle on its slightly stronger legs. As the child learns more, it moves further from its mother. This is an important stage. The child sometimes fears this separation and clings to its mother.

► This young child is getting to know the world she lives in by feeling, holding, tasting and throwing almost everything she comes across. At this age, children learn most things by discovering them for themselves.

▲ *Children building a house out of rugs. Playing make-believe allows children to act out their fantasies and to develop their imagination.*

All babies are different. Some develop faster than others. Some reach one stage quickly and then seem to take a very long time to achieve the next. A small child will walk only when it is ready to do so. What is important is the attitude of its parents. If they love and support the baby, it will feel safe enough to develop quickly. It will take risks and be adventurous.

SOME STAGES IN A BABY'S DEVELOPMENT

One month A baby can lift its head when it's held to someone else's shoulder
Three months It can hold its head steady if it's held to someone's shoulder
Four months It tries to sit up when lying on its back
Five months It rolls from its back to its stomach
Six months It can sit up for a moment if placed against something to lean on
Eight months It can raise itself to a sitting position
Nine months It can sit without support
Ten months It pulls itself to a standing position
Twelve months It can stand with support and walk with help
Fifteen months It can walk and stand alone
Eighteen months It can climb stairs or onto a chair and enjoys scribbling
Two years It can run and play a simple game of catch
Two and a half years It can go up and down stairs alone and can build something with 7 or 8 blocks.
Three years It can copy a drawing of a circle

It can often be difficult to recognize familiar objects when they are shown from an unfamiliar angle. Did you guess that this is a close-up view of pineapple skin?

Learning to See

Learning how to see things involves far more than just learning how to use your eyes. It also involves learning how to make sense of the things the eyes and the brain tell us we are seeing. This is called *perception*.

A newly born baby's eyes and brain function perfectly well. However, if it looks around its hospital room it cannot perceive it—that is, see and understand it—as its mother can. Because it has only just been born, it has almost no experiences to which it can relate what it sees. Babies soon begin to recognize their parents' faces and brightly-colored objects such as mobiles.

Perception is a matter of relating what we see to the many other occasions on which we have seen the same object. We know that we are looking at a chair whether we see it from the front or the back, or from the side, or from above or below. The images of the chair that our retina absorb may well be different depending on where we stand. Nevertheless, we know that we are looking at a chair.

IS SEEING BELIEVING?

▲ Your brain may tell you that this is a drawing of a dog. In fact it is a group of 22 blobs arranged in such a way that you perceive it as a dog.

▶ How many colors appear in this drawing? Your brain may tell you there are four. In fact there are only three. The center circles are the same color. The different colors of the outer circles appear to change that of the inner one.

▲ The way things are arranged affects the way the mind perceives them. You probably see the top row as parallel lines with an extra line at each end, but the bottom row as broken squares.

▶ What size are the center circles in these two drawings? One seems smaller than the other because of the other circles nearby, but in fact they are the same size.

Similarly, people on the opposite side of the street appear to be the same size as people on our own side, although the images we receive of them are smaller. Our brain automatically organizes the images it receives in such a way that what we perceive makes sense to us.

Illusions

The brain is often deceived, however. At night, for instance, what we think is one thing often turns out to be something quite different. The images it casts on the retina are so weak that the brain misunderstands them. Sometimes, too, objects can give out conflicting images. Is the picture at the bottom of this page of a vase or of two faces?

Sometimes the brain can be deceived. Have you ever noticed how large the moon looks when it rises behind trees or houses? When it is high in the sky it looks smaller because there is nothing with which to compare it.

At first glance the picture on the right seems quite normal, because the mind is used to taking account of the size and distance of objects. Only a closer look reveals that the artist has tricked the mind.

▲ This illusionist painting by the Dutch artist Maurits Escher defies the normal world and makes water appear to flow uphill.

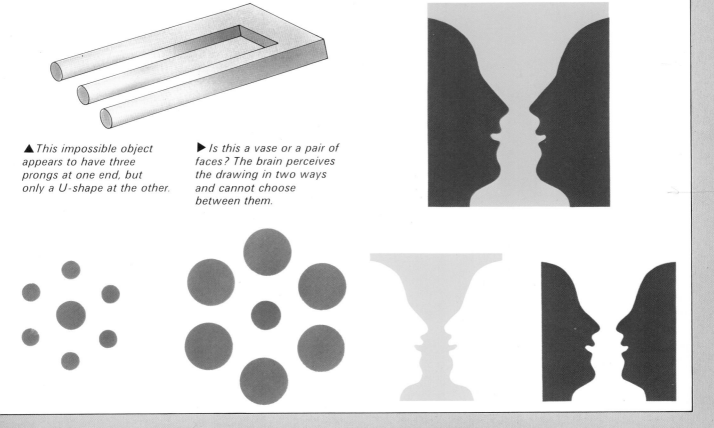

▲ This impossible object appears to have three prongs at one end, but only a U-shape at the other.

▶ Is this a vase or a pair of faces? The brain perceives the drawing in two ways and cannot choose between them.

▼ The ability to reason develops slowly and in separate stages. Young children are unable to grasp certain concepts which seem obvious to older children.

▲ Practice is an important part of learning. This juggler has spent many hours practicing his act until he has perfected every part of it.

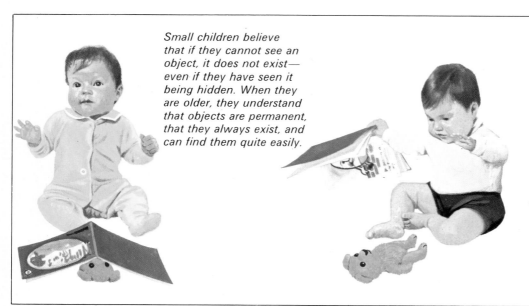

Small children believe that if they cannot see an object, it does not exist— even if they have seen it being hidden. When they are older, they understand that objects are permanent, that they always exist, and can find them quite easily.

▶ It takes children several years to understand the concept of number. Most five-year-olds think there are the same number of blocks in each of the rows on the right. But most of them think there are more in the second row below, just because they are more spaced out.

Learning

Learning begins from the moment of birth. If a baby is picked up when it cries, it soon learns to cry when it wants to be picked up. How we react to a situation often depends on what has happened to us before in similar situations. Most of the time we are not aware of this, but as the mind develops, we can deliberately use past experiences to form new thoughts and ideas, and to learn new skills.

We learn in many different ways.

Trial and error

Trial and error is one of the simplest ways of learning. A baby picks up and shakes every object it can get hold of. With most of them, nothing happens. Then it shakes a rattle and finds to its astonishment that a noise results.

We go on using this method of learning throughout our lives. If you have a bunch of keys and don't know which one fits, you try them all until you find the one that opens the door.

Experience

Life would be difficult and time-consuming if every problem had to be solved by trial and error. Instead, the brain remembers the results of the trial and error experiments. Thus, if the baby wants to make a noise, it very soon realizes that it must pick up its rattle, not some other toy. And you look through a bunch of keys searching for the right sort of key to fit a particular lock, remembering what you used on a previous occasion to open the same kind of lock.

Imitation

You can also learn by imitating someone else. Children learn to talk by imitating the noises they have heard around them since they were born. The first words they learn to say are often "no" and "dadda". This is because these words are easy to imitate, not because they particularly want to use those words rather than any others.

Practice

Practice is closely linked to imitation. If you learn a foreign language from a phonograph record you use both techniques. You hear someone speaking French and then imitate her until you can pronounce the word correctly. You learn to swim by imitating the strokes your instructor shows you and then by practicing them in the water.

The growth of reason

All these types of learning come together to help us to think, or reason, about problems of all kinds. A good driver, for instance, has learned his road skills by imitating his instructor, by practicing how to use the controls, and by experience collected from all the previous occasions on which he has driven a car.

It takes a long time to learn how to reason. Young babies do not realize that people and things do not "disappear" when they cannot see them. The ability to think in purely abstract terms only comes after other basic concepts have been grasped, much later—probably between the ages of 11 and 14.

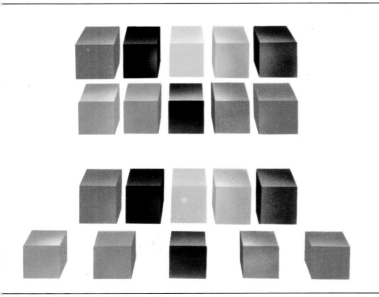

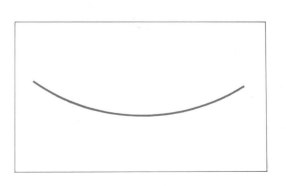

▲ Most people think that if the curved line were straightened out, its ends would reach the edge of the box. Use a piece of string or thread to find out where they do come to. Both adults and children find this idea very hard to grasp.

Memory

TEST YOUR MEMORY

8 6 5 4 2

9 5 1 8 6 9 2 3

3 4 9 6 5 2 7 1 8 2 5

4 5 1 6 8 3 2 4 9 1 6 3 0 7

How good is your short-term memory? Look at each set of figures or words for about 20 seconds, then cover them up and see how many you can remember. The ones that make most sense are usually easiest to recall.

the black and white cat stole
the fish from the pan and ate
it all

dog bit rat but not yet brown
dog long but hog what rat all had

man yet up not cot big long said
hair rain bit red can hat what

Look at the objects below for about half a minute. Then cover them up and see how many you can remember. Try this test on your friends and family too. Short-term memory becomes worse as you grow older. Children of about eleven probably have the best short-term memories.

Our memories are a huge storehouse, full of the things that have happened to us throughout our lives. Every kind of experience can be included: people we have met, events, information we have learned at school and so on.

Scientists disagree about whether our memories retain everything that has ever happened to us, or whether some things do get forgotten. We do remember far more than we can ever recall, however. This means that when we say we have a bad memory, we really mean that we are not very good at recalling things, that is at bringing them from the memory to the front of our minds again. It is often easier to recognize something, than to recall it.

Short-term and long-term memories

There are two types of memory. One retains information for a short period of time. The other is a permanent store.

The amount a long-term memory can store is unlimited. When we talk about what we "know", we are almost always referring to the contents of our long-term memory. Events in our past life and every kind of skill are also kept in the long-term memory.

The short-term memory works in a different kind of way. The amount of information it can contain is limited. We use it to remember information we have just learned, such as the name of someone we have met for the first time. After a time, we either forget the new information or pass it to the long-term memory.

Forgetting and remembering

Since the memory is so good, why do people forget things? Information stored in the short-term memory is forgotten because other information received later pushes it out of the way. Information in both memories may also be forgotten because we repress it. Because it is connected with something unpleasant in our lives, we subconsciously fail to remember it.

Most information is never forgotten, however. It is simply not recalled. What, then, makes us able to recall some things and not others?

Cues help us to improve our powers of recollection. They are called cues because they help to prompt us. They help the mind to make sense of the information it stores. Some *cues* may be in the form of mental pictures. Others may help to organize the material in such a way that makes it easier to recall, for example by rhyming: In 1492 Columbus sailed the ocean blue. Rehearsing information—that is, repeating it over and over again—also helps to make it easier to recall later.

▼ When people say they have a poor memory, they really mean they find it difficult to recall things. Sometimes they first recall something which is part of or close to the name they are trying to remember.

▲ Old people can often remember the distant past more easily and clearly than the present. Everyone finds that mementos such as photographs and souvenirs help them to recall past events.

REMEMBERING AND FORGETTING

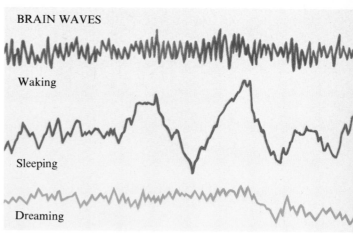

Spending a night in a sleep laboratory. The wires record the sleeper's brain waves and any movements she makes while asleep. The chart above shows the different wave patterns for waking, sleeping and dreaming. By studying such recordings, scientists try to find out more about sleep.

Sleep and Dreams

Most people sleep for about 7 or 8 hours every night. This may seem to be a waste of time. In fact, sleep is very important. It gives the body and mind time to rest and recover their energy.

When you are asleep, the temperature of your body drops and your heart beats more slowly. But your body is not totally inactive. The pituitary gland releases more of the growth hormones during sleep. This is one of the reasons why babies and children need more sleep than adults. People who are ill also sleep more. This gives their bodies time and energy to fight off invading germs and renew damaged tissue.

Dreams

There are two kinds of sleep, orthodox and paradoxical. Dreams take place during paradoxical sleep. Orthodox sleep takes up about 80% of each night's sleep, paradoxical sleep 20%.

Everybody's sleep follows a similar pattern. A period of about 90 minutes of orthodox sleep comes first. This is followed by 10 to 30 minutes of paradoxical sleep. The two kinds of sleep continue to alternate throughout the night, although the periods of paradoxical sleep get longer. Each type of sleep recurs about five times a night.

Although the body is less active than usual during sleep, the brain is not. Nerve impulses continue to move about in it, although they do not receive any new information from the sensory nerves. During dreams the brain is particularly active, sending out different patterns of electrical signals. The eyes dart about rapidly, although the eyelids stay closed, and the muscles relax completely. We only remember dreams if we wake during a period of paradoxical sleep.

No one knows exactly why we dream or what happens during dreams. Many people think that they are a way of sorting out and reacting to events in our waking life. Anything can happen in a dream. Fragments of the day's experience may be linked with people and events we thought we had long forgotten. The mind may wander at random, making impossible connections.

We do know that dreaming is essential. If people are woken up every time they are about to enter a period of paradoxical sleep, they become very unsettled. After two or three days they start to have hallucinations, a kind of waking dream. And if you do go without sleep for a night or two, when you finally sleep again you dream much more than normal.

Insomnia

There is no rule about how much sleep you should get. Some people need less than others. A few can make do with as few as three or four hours a night. People also tend to need less sleep as they get older.

People who find it difficult to get to sleep or stay asleep are said to suffer from insomnia. Sleeping pills can help them to sleep, but they often have bad side effects and make people taking them dream less than normal.

Sleepwalking

Occasionally a person may walk while they are still asleep. People do this during a period of non-dreaming sleep, when they are almost awake.

Sleepwalkers move clumsily, bumping into furniture. Their eyes may be open but glazed, and they may mutter to themselves. Unless they wake up, they rarely remember anything about it the next day. Waking up a sleepwalker will not harm him.

Sleep talking

Sometimes people suddenly sit up in bed and shout! Some people talk in their sleep, repeating phrases they used during the day, or talking complete nonsense. These people rarely remember what they have said next morning.

Snoring

Snoring usually disturbs other people but not the sleeper, although some people snore so loudly that they wake themselves up too. People snore during both kinds of sleep. If they sleep with their mouths open, the air they breathe may vibrate their throat muscles and soft palate. The only way to stop someone snoring is to wake them up.

Yawning

When you are tired or bored, you may start to yawn. Being in a stuffy room may also make you yawn. Yawning helps your body to take in more air and so more oxygen. Oxygen in the blood keeps your brain alert and you awake. Yawning is infectious. If one person starts, others near them soon follow.

▲ The painting "I and My Village" by Marc Chagall may remind you of dreaming. The images overlap and may seem confused.

Mind over Body

People have known for a long time that the mind and body are closely linked. If you are feeling ill, you may also feel fed up and miserable. If you get a sudden shock, the adrenal glands release adrenalin into the body, so making your heart beat faster.

Many people, particularly in the East, have found that by "emptying their mind" and quietening their bodies, they can achieve a state of restful alertness. Their heart beats more slowly, the temperature of their body drops, and their senses become more acute. There are several ways of achieving this state, including yoga, meditation and biofeedback.

Paranormal

Some people claim, and there is some evidence, that the mind has powers outside the normal range of the senses. These powers are called paranormal. Until recently, much of the evidence was unreliable. Some of it was proved to be fraudulent. Recently, many properly controlled experiments have been conducted. Nowadays, most scientists, though not all, say that paranormal events are not impossible, though they also say that they cannot be proved. One reason is that all our methods of proof have been devised for normal events.

Extra-sensory perception

One of the most important types of paranormal phenomena, or happenings, is extra-sensory perception (ESP). There are several different kinds of ESP. ESP involves perceiving something without using the sense organs.

Telepathy is the transfer of thought from one person's mind to that of another person. One experiment often tried is when one person thinks hard about an object in the hope that a second person will be able to conjure up the same object in his mind.

It is important to remember the difference between telepathy and coincidence. Circumstances sometimes make it quite likely that two people will think about the same thing at the same time. And people who know each other very well—husband and wife, for instance, or brother and sister—often think in the same way.

▲ Colin Evans, a medium, floating five meters (16.4 ft) off the ground during a meeting in London in 1937. The photograph is blurred around his feet, because the flash disturbed his concentration, causing him to drop.

▶ Testing telepathy under scientific conditions. The person being tested tries to guess which shape will light up next. Her guess is recorded on the computer. The ESP machine selects the shapes automatically, so there is no chance of fraud or error.

Other forms of ESP are clairvoyance and precognition. Clairvoyance is the power of seeing, without using the eyes, events taking place far away or in another time—the past or the future. Precognition is when someone sees or feels that something they could not know about is about to happen—and it does!

Psychokinesis

Some people are able to control physical objects with their minds. This is called psychokinesis (PK). In one famous experiment in Russia, a woman made small objects move about the top of a table without touching them. She even made an egg break open, separated the white and yolk and then put them back together again. Poltergeists, a type of ghost that haunts a house, making weird noises and throwing objects about, are a form of PK.

Life after death

People who believe that life continues after death, and who are anxious to question a dead relative, sometimes try to get in touch with them through a medium. A medium is a person through whom the spirits of dead people speak. The spirits sometimes answer questions and give advice. Many mediums have been exposed as hoaxers.

▲ Uri Geller is famous for his ability to bend spoons and other pieces of metal simply by stroking them. Some magicians claim to be able to do this too, but no one has ever proved that Geller is a fraud.

► Hypnosis, or suggestion, can produce amazing results. This girl, who has been hypnotized, is able to support the full weight of a man, although she is only resting on her neck and heels. If you look carefully though, you can see that the hypnotist has his hands resting on the girl's knee and shoulder joints (see page 13), so that the structure of her skeleton is giving him support. Nevertheless, sitting on someone like this can be dangerous. Hypnosis can be used medically to help people give up smoking and with other similar problems.

► *A group of friends. Friendships with people of similar age and interests are important throughout life.*

▼ *Exchanging a baton in a relay race. You often compete with people you know, as well as helping or cooperating with them.*

Chapter Seven

Yourself and Others

The previous chapters in this book have described how the body and the mind function, and how we gradually learn to use them. But nobody lives in a vacuum. Everything we do and say brings us into contact with other people, whether they are part of our families, or friends, or colleagues at work or at school. And what they do and say in turn influences our feelings and ideas.

So, apart from learning how to walk, for instance, we also learn to understand ourselves and other people, and how to live with them in society. This is a gradual process which goes on during childhood and adolescence, probably without our even realizing it. In fact, it continues all our life, since our emotions and ideas, and those of other people, go on changing all the time.

The process involves understanding our feelings and also how and when to control them. We gradually learn how to demand and get what we want while considering other people's needs at the same time. We learn how to communicate, not only how to speak and read and write, but how to understand all the subtle aspects of body language that also help to convey meaning.

A child first becomes familiar with the people he sees every day, usually other members of his family. They help him as he begins to explore more of the outside world. Friends also play an important part in influencing him as he grows and becomes more independent of his family.

Each of us develops a unique personality. We may all work inside in the same way. Our external differences of appearance may only be skin deep. But we all react to the world in a different way and have something special to contribute to it.

Feelings and Emotions

Laughing

People laugh when they find something funny, and sometimes when they are nervous and are not sure what to do. When you laugh you breathe in deeply and then breathe out in short spasms, tightening your vocal cords at the same time.

Crying

Crying takes place in much the same way as laughter, although it expresses a very different emotion. Tears are produced all the time. They are important because they bathe the eyes and keep them moist. Crying simply increases the supply, as does laughter, coughing, peeling strong onions, a cold wind, dust in the eye, vomiting and yawning.

▼ *The expressions and attitudes of the people in this scene show anger, resentment, happiness, interest, boredom and cheerfulness. These are just some of the many emotions you can experience.*

Everyone has feelings and emotions. We experience them all the time, although they are stronger at some moments than at others. Yet no one knows exactly what they are or how they are formed. You can recognize when someone is angry or happy, but you cannot actually point to their anger or happiness.

Feelings are often a response to the outside world. Showing that you are angry is both a way of expressing your feelings and also of trying to change someone else's ideas or behavior. Feelings are closely connected with thinking. What we think may make us angry or happy, and feelings of anger or happiness also influence our decisions.

Emotions develop in the brain and the autonomic nervous system. But they are closely linked with the rest of the body. Hunger or tiredness, for instance, can affect our feelings a great deal. If something goes wrong when we are very tired we may react far more violently than if we are quite relaxed.

Emotions can have physical effects, too. If we get angry or excited, the body works itself up by pumping out extra supplies of adrenalin.

Pleasure and displeasure

Feelings and emotions can be put into two groups, those expressing pleasure and those expressing displeasure. Strong feelings of pleasure include joy, love, gratitude and happiness. Strong feelings of displeasure include anger, fear, envy, loneliness, grief and boredom. Sometimes our feelings may conflict. We may, for example, feel gratitude and anger at the same time.

Controlling our feelings

Learning to understand and control feelings is part of growing up.

Almost the only way in which babies can communicate with other people is by expressing their emotions. They laugh and smile when they are happy and contented, and cry when they are frightened or uncomfortable. Young children also express themselves through their emotions a great deal, although they may be able to talk quite fluently. If a child continually behaves badly, this may be its way of expressing feelings of unhappiness.

As we grow older, we gradually learn how to control our emotions. This is because we slowly begin to understand why we sometimes feel the way we do.

Communication

Communication means expressing information, ideas and emotions to other people. If we could not communicate, life would be impossible. We would have no way of finding out about other people or of telling them about ourselves.

Speech

Speech is one of the most important ways of communicating. It consists of far more than just making noises. To talk and also to be understood by other people, we have to speak a language. That is, we have to use combinations of sounds that everyone agrees stand for a particular object or idea. Communication would be impossible if everyone made up their own language.

All small babies make the same sounds, but they learn to speak the language they constantly hear spoken around them. A baby first manages to say individual words, though it may not always understand what they mean. After that it learns to put a few words together and finally it succeeds in speaking in fully formed sentences. This complicated process only takes about three or four years.

Learning a language properly is very important. The basic vocabulary of English is not very large, and only about 2000 words are needed to speak it quite well. But the more words you

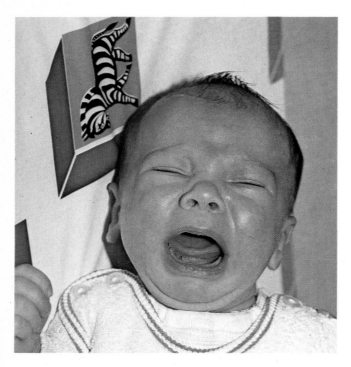

▲ Yelling and screaming is almost the only way babies have of expressing their emotions.

DEVELOPMENT OF LANGUAGE

▼ When young children first learn the word "Dadda", for example, they may use it to stand for all men. A bit later they can distinguish between different men, and later still they can link two words, such as Dadda and juice, to show what they want. When they are about three, they may begin to use short sentences, such as "Dadda give me juice."

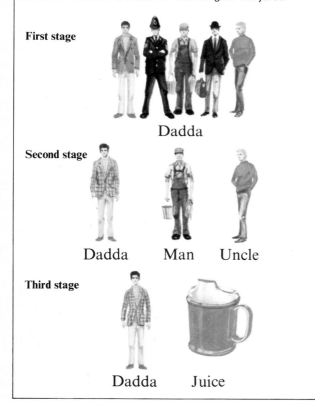

First stage

Dadda

Second stage

Dadda   Man   Uncle

Third stage

Dadda   Juice

USING SIGN LANGUAGE

know, the more ideas you can express, and the more precise you can be about their exact meaning.

Words are the main thing we use in communicating what we want to say. The way we say the words is also very important. Our tone of voice can express many emotions and shows whether we are pleased or angry, for instance. So too can the speed at which we talk, how loudly or softly we talk and the pitch of our voices—that is, how high or low they are. All these things help to make our meaning clearer.

Gestures

As well as talking with our voices, we also talk with our bodies. This may seem surprising at first, but if you watch two people having a conversation you will soon see that it is true. People often move their hands to emphasize what they are saying and to show the person listening to them that they are saying something important. Listeners use gestures too. They may nod their head to show that they have understood or shake it to indicate disagreement.

Many other gestures can be used either as part of a conversation or on their own. If you are really angry with someone, you may show it by clenching your fist and waving it in front of him without saying a single word. Eyebrows too are very expressive. Fully raised, they indicate disbelief, half-raised surprise, half-lowered puzzlement, fully-lowered anger.

Body language

People also express themselves in the way they walk and in their posture—that is, in the way they carry their body. A self-confident person may well look straight ahead and hold his body erect, whereas a nervous person may stoop slightly and look from side to side. And if you are enjoying talking to someone, you tend to sit forward in your seat. If you are not, you may sit back with your arms folded.

All these body signs are a very important part of communication. This is why actors study and practice them a great deal. To play a part on a stage really well, an actor must act as the character would—that is move, and gesture and speak like him—not merely learn his lines. And if you have ever heard someone say of somebody that "You never know what he's thinking", this usually means that he does not communicate what he is thinking through body language.

▼ Marcel Marceau, the famous French mimic. Mime is a very elaborate form of sign language in which ideas are shown without a word being spoken.

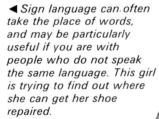

◀ Sign language can often take the place of words, and may be particularly useful if you are with people who do not speak the same language. This girl is trying to find out where she can get her shoe repaired.

Personality

If we describe someone's personality, we are really describing the way that person appears to everyone else. Our description sums up the way he looks and talks and moves, the ideas and feelings he has, the interests he follows—in fact everything about him.

Just because someone has, say, a cheerful personality, this doesn't mean that she has to be cheerful all the time. She can experience the entire range of emotions. We see her as a happy or carefree type only because she often seems to us to be like that.

Personality begins to show very early on in life. Babies react to what happens around them in their own way. As they grow older, they also make sense of the world, also in their own way. Their experiences help to form their personality. They learn how to control themselves, and how to fit in with others. Most manage this without much difficulty, but some habits and moods become a regular part of their personality.

In the Middle Ages, people believed that there were four types of people—sanguine, phlegmatic, choleric and melancholic. Which you were was determined by which of the four main body fluids you had most of—blood, phlegm, yellow bile and black bile. Modern scientists have long since recognized that there is no evidence for this. But the four categories do correspond roughly with some modern theories that group people according to how outgoing (extravert/introvert) and how easily upset (stable/unstable) they are.

These illustrations show how a medieval artist depicted the four different types.

▲ People with a phlegmatic temperament were calm and unexcitable. Today they might be called stable introverts.

▶ People with a sanguine temperament were optimistic and good-natured. Today they might be called stable extraverts.

▲ To many people, fishing might seem to be a sport for introverts: fishermen spend much of their time alone, and even in a contest rarely talk to one another. Yet many fishermen like to spend their evenings with other people, perhaps relating stories of the huge fish they have caught! Labels such as introvert and extravert are not always as useful as they may seem: most people are a mixture of both.

FIND OUT ABOUT YOUR PERSONALITY

Look at the eight colors below. Decide which one you like best. Write down the color and then cover its circle. Which of the remaining colors do you like best? Write it down and cover it up. Repeat until you have covered all of the colors. Write 1st pair beside the first two colors you chose, 2nd pair beside the next two, and so on. You should have four pairs. Now look at the color box on the right to find out what your colors mean. The meanings given there have been very simplified and must not be taken seriously.

◀ *People with a choleric temperament were impatient and quickly become angry. Today they might be called extraverted and unstable.*

▼ *People with a melancholic temperament were pessimistic. Today they might be called introverted and unstable.*

Assessing personality

If you are trying to help someone decide what kind of job to take, or what subjects to study, it can often be helpful to have an idea of his personality. It is no good, for instance, suggesting to someone who is very shy that he should take a job in which he has to meet a lot of people.

Personality tests

Scientists have devised many different kinds of test that try to determine personality. To get a reasonably accurate answer, a long and subtle test is necessary. One such test is based on choosing colors like those shown below. There are over 40,000 different ways of putting these colors in order of preference. Each way indicates a different kind of personality. It takes an entire book to give the proper interpretations. The interpretations, or meanings, given here are very rough. They have been given only for fun and should not be taken seriously.

Interpreting the Color Test

Each color means something different according to whether it is in the first pair of colors you chose, or in the second pair, the third pair, or the fourth pair.
The following tells you the "meaning" of each color for each position.
BLUE in the 1st pair means seeking peace and quiet. In 2nd pair: acts calmly. In 3rd pair: not closely involved. In 4th pair: won't relax.
GREEN in 1st pair: wants to be independent. In 2nd pair: persistent, demands what he wants. In 3rd pair: feels should make the best of things. In 4th pair: unwilling to take steps to overcome stress.
RED in 1st pair: seeking activity and enjoyment. In 2nd pair: active but feels is not making enough progress. In 3rd pair: in need of peace and quiet. In 4th pair: feels helpless.
YELLOW in 1st pair: seeking a change for the better. In 2nd pair: attracted by anything new. In 3rd pair: hopeful but needs reassurance. In 4th pair: has unfulfilled hopes and disappointments.
GRAY in 1st pair: unwilling to join in or feels exhausted. In 2nd pair: having difficulty in getting desires. In 3rd pair: willing to join in but avoids conflict. In 4th pair: impatient.
VIOLET in 1st pair: yearns for romantic tenderness. In 2nd pair: needs to express himself sensitively. In 3rd pair: quick to take offense. In 4th pair: controlled and demands sincerity.
BROWN in 1st pair: seeks freedom from problems and wants relaxation. In 2nd pair: feels uneasy and insecure. In 3rd pair: sensual. In 4th pair: demands esteem from others.
BLACK in 1st pair: considers existing circumstances are disagreeable and demanding. In 2nd pair: dissatisfied. In 3rd pair: feels that things stand in his way. In 4th pair: wants to be independent.

PHOBIAS

From time to time, most people feel afraid of things that are not really dangerous or threatening. Children, for instance, are afraid of the dark. Other people fear spiders or heights or crowds of people. Although they know that nothing terrible is going to happen, they cannot stop getting scared.

These unreal fears are called phobias. Other phobias include fear of lifts, moths, birds, snakes, even of going outside. Why should people be afraid of something they know cannot really harm them? The answer is that their phobia stands for something they fear but do not want to think about. The phobia hides the real fear, even from themselves.

► *Close ties of love develop between parents and children almost from the moment they are born. This is partly because parents are with their children all the time and give them all they need.*

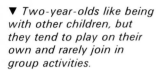

▼ *Two-year-olds like being with other children, but they tend to play on their own and rarely join in group activities.*

► *Five-year-olds of both sexes enjoy playing together. Often one child—perhaps the oldest or the most self-confident—will take the lead.*

◄ *Between the ages of about seven and twelve, many children prefer to play only with other children of the same sex. They often form close-knit groups, absorbed in their own activities.*

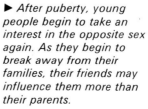

► *After puberty, young people begin to take an interest in the opposite sex again. As they begin to break away from their families, their friends may influence them more than their parents.*

Making Friends

Making friends and keeping them is a two-way process. To do it successfully, you have to be interested in other people. You also have to be confident enough yourself to let someone else take part in your life.

Babies and young children are not mature enough to do this. The first years of their life are spent exploring the world and developing their abilities. They tend to experience people and things as being part of themselves. They rely on their parents to provide them with food, warmth and love, but are not very curious about other people.

When they are about three years old, children usually become much more interested in other people. They begin to learn to accommodate other people. This process takes just as long as every other part of a child's mental and physical development and, in fact, goes on throughout life.

Groups and gangs

From about the age of three, children often enjoy playing in groups. At first these groups are very loosely formed. The people who belong to them change frequently, and both girls and boys are members.

▶ Some friendships or flirtations may become more important and develop into love.

After a few years, perhaps around the age of eight, these groups—or gangs as they may be called—change their nature. Membership is confined to one sex and it is often very strictly controlled. The group does a lot of things together and are very loyal to one another. One member comes to be respected by all the others and becomes the gang leader. He gains that respect because he understands what the others want and admire, and manages to express those things for them. As children become adolescents, their group of friends tends to include people of both sexes.

Individual friendships

As well as being part of a group of friends, most children usually have one or two "best" friends whom they see more often. At first, these are usually people of the same sex. Later, they may also be with people of the opposite sex. Some friendships may develop into love affairs.

All the stages described here are generalizations. This means that they are what usually takes place. What actually happens to individual people, and when it happens, varies a great deal. Some people seem to have many friends while others have just a few people to whom they feel close. But most people consider that their friends are important. They share ideas and interests. And in crises they can give help and advice, sometimes more effectively than a family member.

◄ A big family reunion covering three generations. The extended family includes aunts, uncles and cousins, as well as grand-parents, brothers, sisters and parents. People who marry members of the family or who are adopted by the family also belong to it.

▼ The same extended family drawn in the form of a family tree.

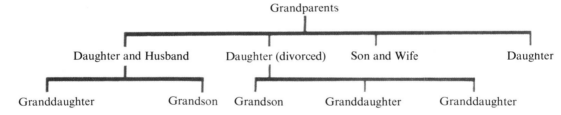

◄ A typical nuclear family consisting of just mother and father and their children. The family tree is shown below.

▶ Teenagers often seem to be at odds with their families—holding long, costly phone conversations is a common cause of trouble!

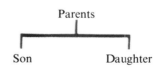

The Family Group

A family is a group of people all of whom are closely related to one another. When people talk about families nowadays, they are usually referring to the nuclear family. This is a small group which consists of two generations—mother and father and their children. Sometimes, though, grandparents may come to live with the basic nuclear family. Rather than being isolated, the grandparents are then able to play a useful role within the family.

The extended family is a term used to describe a much larger family group. It can include uncles and aunts, nieces and nephews, cousins, perhaps even great-grandparents.

Nowadays, most people, at least in the Western world, live together as a nuclear family. Often, at least some other members of their extended family may live nearby. It is quite usual, though, for some parts of the extended family to live hundreds of miles away or even in a different country.

Some nuclear families have only one parent. They are called single-parent families. The other parent may have died, or perhaps the parents never married, or decided to split up and become divorced.

What is a family for?

One of the main purposes of a family is to bring up children. A mother and father care for each child from the moment it is born. At first, while it is still a tiny baby, they have to do everything for it. Later, as it begins to grow up, they help and encourage it to explore the world around it.

Families are important for children of all ages, however. Parents, and brothers and sisters and grandparents, all play an important part in the process of growing up. Even when children rebel against everything their parents believe in during adolescence, the family remains important to them, if only as something to break away from.

Until fairly recently, fathers went to work to earn money and mothers stayed at home and looked after the house and family. Nowadays, however, many women want to earn money themselves and to follow their own career. Fathers, too, want to take a much larger part in looking after their children. As a result, in many families both parents work and share the domestic work when they get home. In a very few, the mother goes out to work while the father stays at home.

A family does not stop functioning just because its children have grown up and left home. They usually visit each other frequently, and family members come together to share both problems and pleasures.

► A father feeding his child. Nowadays, many fathers regularly help to do the housework and look after the children.

FACT INDEX

Most of the entries in this Fact Index are followed by one or more page numbers. These refer you to pages in the book where there is information about the entry. A few entries contain information only and are not followed by page numbers. Words printed in *italic* type refer you to other index entries that you should read. Page numbers in **bold** type indicate illustrations. Some of the more important entries have a lot of page references. You may also find it useful to look at the contents list at the beginning of the book if you want to find out whether one of these entries is discussed at length.

A

Adenoids are part of the lymphatic system and help to fight disease **40**

Adolescence is the period between childhood and adulthood. *Puberty* is the physical aspect of adolescence 33, 79, 85, 87, **87**

Adrenalin, hormone produced in the adrenal glands **60**, 61, 74, 79

Adrenal glands 58, **59**

Allergy An allergy is an abnormal physical reaction to something—a type of food or a drug, for instance—that most people find harm-

less. Usually, the body produces *antibodies* only when it is infected by germs. However, people who suffer from an allergy to grass pollen start to manufacture antibodies as soon as the pollen enters their body. The antibodies produce a reaction, in this case an attack of hay fever. Allergies can, however, have both physical and psychological causes.

Alveoli, tiny air sacs in the lungs where oxygen passes into the blood, and carbon dioxide leaves the blood 22

Amnesia Sudden loss of memory due to excessive stress or to an accident. The loss of memory is usually only temporary and may concern only the events which caused it. 25

Anaesthetics are drugs given to avoid pain. They affect the *nervous system* so that incoming sensory information is temporarily stopped. Local anaesthetics have an effect on the *sensory nerves* in one part of the body only. They are often used by dentists. A general anaesthetic affects the whole nervous system. The patient becomes unconscious for a time. It is often given before an operation.

Antibiotics are drugs used to fight an infectious disease. They attack *bacteria* without harming the *cells* of the patient's body. They are usually taken as tablets or given as an injection. 41

Bacteria are tiny specks of living matter. They are so small that it would take millions to cover the head of a pin. They live on the inside and outside of the body. Most bacteria are harmless. When the harmful ones infect the body, it uses

Blindness
Blindness means an absence of useful sight. Only people whose *optic nerves* or eyes have been injured and completely damaged can see no light at all. Most blind people in richer countries are old people whose eyesight has gradually grown worse. A few babies are born blind. They may have inherited the defect or been injured during *pregnancy*. Blindness caused by disease is much more common in poor countries than in the richer countries.

white blood cells and antibodies to destroy them. 42, **42**

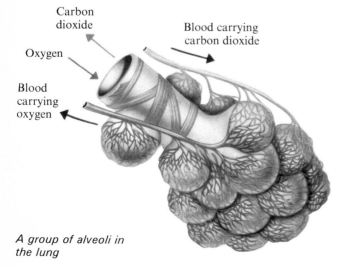

Carbon dioxide

Oxygen

Blood carrying oxygen

Blood carrying carbon dioxide

A group of alveoli in the lung

Bones 12, **12**, **13**, **14**, 34, **34**
Brain 20, 21, 34, 46, 49, 50, **50**, 51, **51**, 53, 54, 55, 58, 61, 63, 66, 67, 72, 79
Brain damage 21, 51
Breasts 33
Bronchi are air passages of the lungs. 22, **22**, 23
Bronchitis is inflammation of the air passages of the lungs, caused by germs or smoking. 36
Bruises 21

C

Caesarian section is the name given to the operation in which doctors open up a mother's *uterus* and lift the baby out when it is ready to be born. The operation is fairly common and is performed if *labor* might harm the baby or mother. 29
Calcium is an important mineral stored in the bones and distributed round the body by the blood. It helps the nerve *cells* and *muscle* fibers to function properly and blood to clot. Calcium is especially important for children, pregnant women and mothers with small children. Too little calcium leads to bad *teeth* and a disease called rickets, in which the bones fail to grow properly. The body obtains its calcium supply from *Vitamin* D (manufactured from sunlight) and from foods such as milk, egg yolks and cheese. 12
Cancer arises when the cells in one part of an adult's body stop renewing themselves in the normal way and start increasing rapidly. This results in a growth, or tumor, which may start to invade the rest of the body. Cancer is one of the most serious diseases in the prosperous Western world, and many people die from it. If the tumor is removed while it is still quite small, however, a full recovery may be made. 35, 36
Canines, a particular kind of *teeth* **18**
Capillaries are the smallest blood vessels. Blood flows from the *arteries* to the capillaries, where it leaves the food and oxygen required by the *cells* and collects the cells' waste products. Then it moves into the *veins* and towards the *heart* again. 20, **20**
Carbohydrates are foods that provide the body with the energy it needs. They

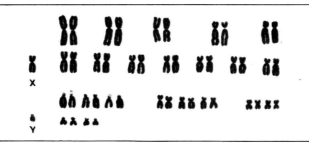

A complete set of male chromosomes. The X and Y chromosomes that make him a man are on the left.

include sugar, potatoes, bread, rice and pasta. 18, 38, **38**
Carbon dioxide 21, 22
Cartilage is a smooth gristle that covers moving parts of the *joints* so that they can move freely and painlessly. Arthritis is a painful disease caused when the cartilage wears away from the joint so that the exposed ends of the bones rub together. 12, **12**, 36
Cells are the smallest living units. Each part of the body consists of millions of identical cells. 34, 35, 43
Cerebellum, part of the brain **56**
Cervix, part of the female *reproductive system* **28**, 29
Choking 19
Chromosomes are made up of *genes*. Every new *cell* that is formed throughout a person's life has the same chromosomes and genes. 30, **30**
Chyme, produced in the stomach, is a mixture of food and *gastric juices*. 18, **19**
Cilia are fine hairs lining the nose and air passages. 22, **56**
Circulatory system is the name used to describe the *arteries*, *capillaries* and *veins* through which the *heart* pumps the blood. 14, **17**, 20, **20**, 21, 29, 39
Clairvoyance 75.
Cochlea, part of the inner ear 54, **55**
Coccyx is the bottom bone of the backbone. It is formed by the fusion of several vertebrae and is all that remains of the tail. **13**
Cold (body temperature) 11, 46, **57**
Cold, inflammation of the nose and throat due to a *virus infection* 42, **42**
Color blindness People who are color blind are unable to distinguish between certain colors, most often red and green. The condition is inherited and is

usually the result of faulty *cones* in the retina. More men are color blind than women. 53
Conception is the moment at which a man's *sperm* fertilizes a woman's *egg* and at which a new life starts to grow. 28, 29, 34
Cones are light receptors in the eye which detect color. 53, **53**
Contact lenses fit directly on to the eyes. They often improve vision far more than ordinary spectacles, but some people find them uncomfortable to wear. **52**, 53
Contraception, prevention of conception by artificial means 28
Contractions occur in the *uterus* during *labor*. 29
Cornea, part of the eye **52**, 53
Corpus callosum, part of the brain **50**
Cortex, part of the brain 50, **50**, 51, **51**
Cortex, outer part of the kidney **24**
Coughing 23
Cramp is a sudden, painful contraction of the *muscles* brought about by the *nervous system*. It can be caused by loss of salt in the body, perhaps as a result of sweating in very hot weather, or by poor circulation. In many cases, however, no one knows why the attack has taken place.
Crying 79
Cues 71, **71**
Curie, Marie (1867–1934) and **Pierre** (1859–1906) were French physicists and chemists who won the Nobel Prize jointly in 1903 for their discovery of radium. The radiation from radium is used to treat *cancer*.

D

Deafness 54
Death 25, 35
Decibel, a measurement of noise **55**

Dermis, the second layer of skin **10**, 11, 25, 57
Diabetes is a disease caused by the body producing too much or too little *insulin*. Diabetics have to inject themselves with insulin every day so that their bodies have the right amount. 36, 58, **58**
Diaphragm controls breathing. It is a sheet of *muscle* between the *lungs* and the *stomach*. **15**, 22, **22**
Diarrhea 19
Diet 36, 38, 39
Digestive juices See *gastric juices*.
Digestive system is the term used to describe those parts of the body through which food travels after it has been eaten. 16, **16**, 18, **19**, 36, 61
Disease 34, 39. 41

These bacteria can cause the disease tetanus, sometimes called lockjaw, if they get into an infected wound.

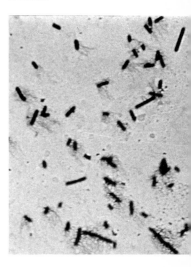

Displeasure See *feelings*.
Dominant gene See *gene*.
Dreams 63, 72, **72**, **73**
Drugs 36, 41
Dumbness See box below.

Dumbness
Children who are born deaf can make sounds but find it difficult to speak, since if you cannot hear other people talking, it is difficult to imitate the sounds they make. "Dumb" children can be taught to speak. Dumbness may also be caused by a *stroke* which affects the muscles of the part of the brain concerned with speech.

Exercise is an important part of staying healthy, but you do not have to have expensive equipment.

E
Eardrum 54, 55
Ears 54, **54**, **55**
EEG (electro-encephalogram) 35
Egg, the female sex cell 28, **30**, 31, 32, **34**
Emotions 50, 76, **78**, 79, 81, 82
Epidermis, the first or outer layer of skin **10**, 11, 57
Epiglottis The epiglottis, a flap made of cartilage, covers the vocal cords as you swallow, and so stops food going down the windpipe. **19**, **22**
Epilepsy 36
Eustachian tube, part of the ear **55**
Exercise 14, 39, **39**, 41, **61**
Extended family includes people who have married into the family or been adopted into it, as well as those who are related by birth. **86**, 87
Extra-sensory perception (ESP) is the term used to describe some people's ability to be aware of something without using their sense organs. 74, 75
Extraverts are said to be sociable, outgoing people. 82
Eyelashes 40, 41
Eyelids 40
Eye 30, **31**, 41, 50, **51**, 53, 66, 67

A lavish selection of food in a hotel. Any well balanced diet provides all the nourishment you need.

F
Fainting 35
Fallopian tubes, part of the female reproductive system 28, **28**
Family 30, 76, **86**, 87. See also *extended family* and *nuclear family.*
Fats provide the body with most of the energy it needs. They either come from animals—fat on meat, milk, eggs—or from vegetable oils. 18, **19**, 38
Feces are the waste products expelled from the *digestive system* through the rectum. 18
Feelings 76, **78**, 79
Fertilization 30, 31
Fetus A fetus is an unborn infant. The word embryo is generally used to describe a fetus between *conception* and the eighth week of *pregnancy.* **28**, 29, 32
Fever 25, 43, **43**
Fingerprints 8
Follicles, small pits in the skin from which hair grows 11, **11**
Food 14, **16**, 18, **19**, 20, 25, 29, 34, 35, 51, 61
Food poisoning 36, 42, **43**
Forgetting 71, **71**
Freckles 11
Friends 76, **77**, **84**, 85, **85**
Frostbite 25
Funeral 35
Fungi poisoning 43. See also *food poisoning.*

G
Gallbladder, an organ just below the liver. It makes and stores bile, releasing it into the duodenum (the first part of the *small intestine*) as food passes through. Bile helps the body to digest *fats.* **18**
Gangs are close-knit groups of friends of about the same age. Gangs are fairly common among pre-adolescent and adolescent children. 85, **85**

Gastric juices enter the *stomach* and the *small intestine* while food is being digested. They help to break the food down, and to kill *germs. Saliva* is also a gastric juice. 18, **19**, 40
Geller, Uri 75
Gene is a unit of hereditary information that helps to decide our characteristics. There are hundreds of genes on each *chromosome.* Each characteristic is decided by several genes. Genes can be either dominant or recessive. If a dominant gene is inherited from one or other parent, it will always show itself. The recessive characteristic only appears if both genes are recessive. 11, 26, **30**, 31, **31**
Germs 11, 23, 36, **40**, 41, 42, 72
Gestures are movements of the face or body to show information or emotion. **80**, 81
Glands Endocrine glands release *hormones* straight into the bloodstream whenever they are needed. Exocrine glands have ducts which carry substances they make, such as sweat or *saliva,* to the part of the body where they are needed (for example, the skin and mouth). 36, 46, 58, **59**
Glucose supplies the body with the energy it needs. It reaches the body's *cells* through the *circulatory system* and is produced by the *digestive system* from *carbohydrates.* The liver also makes glucose from *proteins* and *fats.* The amount of glucose the body uses is controlled by a hormone, *insulin,* which is produced by the *pancreas.*
Glottis, the gap between the vocal cords 23, **23**
Goose pimples 25
Growing up 26, 32, **32**, 33, **33**, 64, 65, **65**, 76, 79, 84, 85, **85**, 87

H
Hair 10, 11, 16, 29, **34**, **59**
Hallucinations 72
Hammer, one of the bones in the middle ear **55**
Hearing 34, **34**, 46, 51, **51**, 54, 55
Hearing aids 45, 54
Heart is a *muscle* which pumps blood around the body. 16, 20, **20**, 21, 29, 35, 36, 39, 43, 61, 74
Heart attack, or heart failure, occurs when the *heart* fails to work properly. 35, 36
Heart pacemaker 45

Heat (body temperature) 25 43, **43**: response to heat 11, 46, 49, **57**
Hiccups 23
Hormones are chemical substances that help to control the working and development of the body. They are released into the bloodstream by the endocrine *glands.* 32, 46, 58, **59**, 72
Hospitals 44, **44**, 45

This hospital patient is receiving intensive care. Machines record his condition and can provide him with food and oxygen.

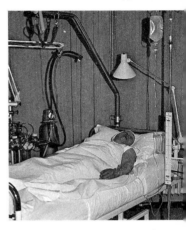

Hunger The feeling of hunger is produced by contractions of the *stomach.* These can occur because the level of sugar in the blood falls, or simply because you expect to eat.
Hygiene is keeping yourself and your surroundings clean. It is an important part of staying healthy. 36, 42
Hypnosis 75
Hypothalamus, part of the brain 50, 51

I
Illusions 66, 67, **67**
Imitation 69
Immunization The body is immune to any disease whose *antibodies* are present in the blood. 36
Incisors, a particular kind of *teeth* 18
Incubation is the period between being infected with a disease and the appearance of its signs and symptoms. Although you do not feel ill during incubation, germs are attacking the body and the *infection* can be passed on to other people. The length of incubation varies greatly from illness to illness. 42, **42**, 43, **43**

Indigestion 19
Infection, invasion of the body by germs 42, **42**, 43
Infectious diseases 35, 36 42, **42**, 43, **43**
Inflammation See box below.
Inheritance Inherited characteristics are those features which are passed on to children through their parents' *genes*. 8, 30, **30**, 31, **31**
Inner ear 54, **55**
Insomnia 72
Insulin is a *hormone* produced in the *pancreas*. It helps the body take sugar from the blood. 58, **58**
Intelligence is the word used to describe a person's ability to reason — that is, their capacity to think and understand. 30, 50, **50**
Intestine See *small intestine, large intestine.*
Introverts are said to be reserved and are happy to be on their own. **82**
Involuntary muscles 14
Iris, part of the eye **52**
Itch 11, 57

J
Joints Two or more bones meet at a joint. There are several different kinds, each of which enables the bones attached to them to move in a different way. 12, **13**, 14, **34**, 36, 55

K
Keratin Hair, nails and the thin, tough outer layer of the skin are made of keratin. 11
Kidney machines 45
Kidneys 16, 24, **24**, 34, 35

L
Labor is the process by which a woman gives birth. 29, **29**

Inflammation
If part of the skin is injured — as a result of an insect bite for example — it swells up and looks red and angry. The damaged *cells* cause the *capillaries* to leak blood and also a watery fluid. The blood makes the injury red and hot, while the fluid makes it swell up. The fluid and the body's *white blood cells* fight the infection and also form a solid clot in the form of a scab. See also *pus*.

Liver
One of the most important functions of the liver is controlling the products of the *digestive system*. Blood containing digested food flows from the *small intestine* to the liver along the hepatic portal vein. The liver then regulates the bloodstream's distribution of the digested food to the rest of the body. It also stores surplus *carbohydrates, proteins, fats* and *vitamins* until they are needed. The liver reduces poisons brought into the body by food, drugs or alcohol. It also produces *bile*.

Lactic acid, waste products produced by the *muscles* as they work 14
Language 23, 80, **80**, 81
Large intestine, part of the *digestive system* 18, **18**, 19
Larynx See *voice box.*
Laughter 78
Learning 64, **65, 68**, 69
Lens, part of the eye 52, 53
Life after death 75
Ligaments hold *joints* together and limit their movement. 12, **12**
Light receptors are the ends of the *sensory nerve* which links the eye to the brain. They consist of *rods* and *cones.* 53
Liver 18, **34**, 38, 40. See also box above.
Lungs 12, 14, 20, **20**, 22, **22**, 23, 35, **60**, 61
Lymph is made up of small amounts of *protein* too large to be absorbed into the bloodstream. Lymph nodes produce *white blood cells* which help to fight disease. Lymph is carried by the lymphatic system, a series of tiny channels that take lymph from *cells* all over the body to two *veins* at the base of the neck, where it joins the bloodstream. 18, **40**

M
Meditation 74
Mediums 74, 75
Medicine is a drug or mixture of drugs given to fight disease. It is also the name given to the study of sickness and health.
Medulla, part of the kidney **24**
Medulla oblongata, part of the brain **50**

Melanin is a substance made in the Malpighian layer of the skin which protects the skin from the harmful ultra-violet rays of the sun. The more melanin there is in the skin, the darker it is. **10**, 11
Membrane is a thin film covering or joining internal parts of the body. **12**
Memory 34, 50, **50**, 51, 63, 70, **70**, 71, **71**
Menstrual cycle 33, **33**
Menstruation 32
Mental deficiency Term used to describe people whose brain has been so damaged (usually before or during birth) that their *intelligence* does not develop a great deal.
Mental illness If people become so disturbed or upset

that they cannot continue with their usual life, they may be said to be mentally ill.
Middle ear 54, **55**
Mime is acting out information through gestures only. **81**
Minerals 38, **38**. See also *calcium.*
Miscarriage A miscarriage takes place when a *fetus* dies in its mother's *uterus*. Most miscarriages happen during the third and fourth months of *pregnancy*. A still birth is the term used when a baby is born dead.
Mnemonics are rhymes or codes which are easy to remember and which represent or help to recall things which are hard to remember.
Molars, a particular kind of *teeth* 18, **19**
Moles 11. See also *birthmark.*
Motor nerves are those nerves that relay messages from the brain to the *muscles* to make them contract. 46, **48**, 49, **49**, 50

Mucus is a clear fluid which protects internal passages. *Infection* increases the supply of mucus. 22, 40, 41
Multiple birth is the term used when two or more children are born at the same time. 8, **31**

Quadruplets from Sarajevo in Yugoslavia. Like twins, triplets, quads and quins can be identical or dissimilar. Twins occur about once every 100 births, triplets about once every 8000 births. Quadruplets occur once in 650,000, quintuplets very rarely — about once in 57 million births.

Muscles are bundles of fibers attached to bones. They can only contract, and do so when a message from the brain reaches them along the *motor nerves.* 12, **12**, 14, **14**, **15**, 20, 21, 25, 33, 34, 36, 39, **46**, 55, 61, **61**

N
Nails 11, 29
Nervous system links the body with the brain. It conducts information collected by the sense organs to the brain and carries messages from the brain to the rest of the body. 14, 36, 46, 48, **48**, 49, 53, 54, 56, 57, 58, 63, 72. See also *motor nerves* and *sensory nerves.*
Neurones are the nerve cells which conduct information in the form of impulses between the brain and the body. 49
Noise 54, 55
Noradrenalin is a *hormone* produced by the adrenal glands. 61
Nose 22, **22**

Many paralyzed people use wheelchairs to get around. With the help of special facilities such as this telephone box, they can live an almost normal life.

Paralysis
Paralysis is the word used to describe total loss of movement in any part of the body. People are usually paralyzed because their brain has been damaged and is no longer able to send messages along the *motor nerves*. Sometimes paralysis is the result of an accident which damaged the nerves leading from one part of the body to the brain.

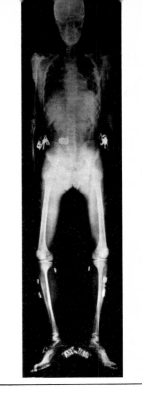

▶ *An X-ray of a man*

Some Vital Statistics
The average person consists of 41% muscle, 16% fat, 14% bone and marrow, 12% internal organs, 9% skin and tissue, and 8% blood.

Hair: The average scalp contains about 100,000 hairs; 30 to 60 are shed every day. On average, about 8 meters (25 ft) of hair is grown during a lifetime, though individual hairs seldom grow more than a meter (3 ft).

Teeth: Adults have up to 32; children have 20.

Bones: Adults have 206; newborn babies have about 350.

Muscles: About 656.

Blood: On average, the body contains 6 liters (10.5 pints) of blood. The blood contains about 25,000,000,000,000 red blood cells, with an average life of 3 to 4 months each; 200,000,000,000 are replaced each day. A single red blood cell which lives 3 months makes about 130,000 round trips from the heart to the rest of the body. The blood also contains between 20 and 50,000,000,000 white blood cells. The circulatory system is about 100,000 km (60,000 miles) long.

Heart: It beats about 70 times a minute and pumps about 9000 liters (2000 gallons) of blood a day. At rest it pumps about 4.5 liters (1 gallon) a minute, but it can increase that amount to about 25 liters (5.5 gallons) if necessary.
If the body is at rest, blood leaving the heart takes 6 seconds to travel to the lungs and back, 8 seconds to the brain and back, 16 seconds to the toes and back.

Digestion: On average, food spends 3 to 5 hours in the stomach, about 4.5 hours in the small intestine, and 5 to 25 hours in the large intestine. The alimentary canal (the entire digestive system) is more than 10 meters (30 feet) long.

Breathing: A minute's breathing provides about 6 liters (10 pints) of air; a day's breathing provides 15,000 liters (3300 gallons). The surface area of the lungs is 70 to 90 square meters (800–1000 sq ft). There are about 300,000,000 alveoli.

Brain and nervous system: The brain has about 14,000,000 cells. Messages travel through the nervous system to and from the brain at 400 kph (250 mph) maximum along the longest fibers. They go much more slowly along shorter fibers.

ACKNOWLEDGEMENTS

Picture Research: Penny Warn, Tracy Rawlings
Photographs: Endpapers ZEFA; Page 4/5 Photri; 6 Allsport/Tony Duffy *right*, Anthea Sieveking *top left*, Barnaby's Picture Library *bottom left*; 9 Syndication International Limited; 10 ZEFA *top left*, *top right*, *center left*, Bermuda Tourist Office *bottom left*; 14 ZEFA; 15 John Watney Photo Library; 23 Michael Chinery; 24/25 Colt International Ltd; 26, 27 ZEFA; 31 Roger Chinery; 35 Paul Popper Ltd; 37 Australian News and Information Bureau; 38 FAO Photo; 39 Photri *top*, Australian News and Information Bureau *bottom*; 41 World Health Organization; 42 Gene Cox *top*, Anthea Sieveking *bottom*; 44 Middlesex Hospital *bottom left*, University of Leeds and United Leeds Hospital *bottom right*; 45 John Watney Photo Library *top left*, Daily Telegraph Colour Library *right*; 47 All Sport/Tony Duffy; 52 LAT; 53 All Sport/Don Morley; 55 Barnaby's Picture Library; 58 World Health Organization; 59 ZEFA *top left*, Paul Popper Ltd *top right*, Ken Merrylees *bottom*; 62 ZEFA; 63 London Transport; 64, 65 Anthea Sieveking; 66 Gene Cox; 67 'The Waterfall' from the Escher Foundation-Haags Gemeentemuseum, The Hague; 68, 71 ZEFA; 72 J.I. Evans; 73 The Museum of Modern Art, New York/Mrs. Simon Guggenheim Fund; 74 Psychic News *bottom left*, Leif Geiges *bottom right*; 75 Syndication International Limited *top*, Radio Times Hulton Picture Library *bottom*; 76 All Sport/Tony Duffy; 77, 80 ZEFA; 81 Joe Bulaitis; 82 Arthur Oglesby; 82/83 The Bettmann Archive Inc.; 83 Daily Telegraph Colour Library; 84 ZEFA *top*, *bottom*, Anthea Sieveking *center*; 84/85 Anthea Sieveking; 85 ZEFA; 86 ZEFA *top*, British Tourist Authority *bottom*; 86/87, 87 Anthea Sieveking; 89 Bruce Coleman Limited; 90 Carnielli *top left*, Savoy Hotel *bottom*, ZEFA *right*; 91 Keystone Press Agency; 92 Paul Popper Ltd; 93 Deutsches Museum, Munich; Cover: ZEFA *top left*, *top right*, Raleigh *bottom left*, John Watney Photo Library *bottom right*, Joe Bulaitis *back*.
Artwork: Tudor Art Agency (Brian Pearce, Norman Cumming, Mike Saunders); Linden Art Agency (Valerie Sangster); Irenè Radó-Vajda. Cover design: Tudor Art Agency.